Returning to Joy

Returning to Joy

A Jewish self-care guide for overcoming depression

RABBI JOSHUA MARK, PH.D.

TARGUM/FELDHEIM

First published 2003
Copyright © 2003 by Joshua Mark
ISBN 1-56871-236-7

All rights reserved

No part of this publication may be translated, reproduced, stored in a retrieval system, or transmitted in any form or by any means, electronic, mechanical, photocopying, recording, or otherwise, without prior permission in writing from both the copyright holder and the publisher.

Published by:
TARGUM PRESS, INC.
22700 W. Eleven Mile Rd.
Southfield, MI 48034
E-mail: targum@netvision.net.il
Fax: 888-298-9992
www.targum.com

Distributed by:
FELDHEIM PUBLISHERS
202 Airport Executive Park
Nanuet, NY 10954

Printed in Israel

Dedication

Returning to Joy is dedicated to

Rav Yehuda Parnes,
who taught me about thinking;

Dr. Chaim Kranzler, M.D.,
who taught me about feelings;

my wonderful wife, Beth,
who taught me about joy.

הוציאה ממסגר נפשי להודות את שמך
בי יכתירו צדיקים כי תגמול עלי.
(תהילים קמ״ב)

Release my soul
from the trap to acknowledge Your name.
The righteous shall use me as a crown to adorn
themselves, for You have granted good to me.
(*Tehillim* 142)

Contents

Foreword 9
About the Title of this Book 11
Acknowledgments 13
Introduction: Why Another Book about Such
　a Depressing Topic? 16

Learning about Depression

1. First Things First: Are You Depressed? 27
2. The Raging Epidemic of Depression 34
3. The Causes of Depression 39

Combating Your Depression

4. Tackling Your Persistently
　Depressed Mood 49
5. Tackling Sleep Problems 77
6. Tackling Appetite Disturbances 91
7. Tackling Hopelessness and Pessimism 98
8. Tackling Increased or
　Decreased Energy. 120
9. Tackling Problems with Concentration,
　Memory, and Racing Thoughts 129

10. Tackling Worthlessness and Guilt 139
11. Tackling Thoughts of Death and Suicide . . . 148
12. Tackling Irritability and Anger 155
13. Shame, Modesty, and Self-Esteem 164
14. Reducing Anxiety. 171
15. Staying on Course 180

Depression and Our Lives

16. Depression in the Observant Family 187
17. Special Concerns for Women 196
18. Special Concerns for Men 201
19. Depression and the Torah-Observant Single . 207
20. The Older Adult and Depression 211

Conclusion: The Gift of Clinical Depression. . . . 217
Appendix A: List of Feelings 221
Appendix B: Antidepressant Medications 224
Appendix C: Electroconvulsive Therapy. 228
Appendix D: Psychosis and Depression 230

For Further Reading. 232

Foreword

The reason for the startling increase in depressive disorders in recent years is unclear, but one thing is very clear: the Jewish population is unfortunately well represented. This population is at a disadvantage, because the stigma attached to emotional disorders among Jews discourages many people from seeking appropriate help. Depressive disorders that are neglected are not only agonizing to the sufferer, but also impact heavily on the family and the community.

In the past it was assumed that depressions occurred only in adults. Recent research has indicated that many youngsters suffer from depression, although the symptoms may differ from the adult depression. In youngsters, depression can be particularly damaging, as it may impair their education and maturation.

Fortunately, great advances have been made in understanding depression, both its physiological and psychological causes. We also have effective therapies, both physiological and psychological. It is simply unconscionable for a person and family to suffer from a condition which is treatable.

Rabbi Joshua Mark has made a major contribution with his book, *Returning to Joy*. He provides not only vital clarification of depression, but also ways in which a person may actually help oneself recover. In those cases where treatment is required, the information in *Returning to Joy* is a valuable adjunct that can increase the effectiveness of treatment and may help prevent recurrences.

Returning to Joy is must reading not only for people who suffer from depression and for their families, but also for people who are free from these disorders. The prevalence of depression today is so great that everyone will benefit in being forearmed with valid information.

In citing many references from Torah literature, Rabbi Mark has indeed had a great mitzvah in presenting important information in a way that will be acceptable to Torah-observant people.

> Rabbi Abraham J. Twerski, M.D.
> Founder and Medical Director Emeritus
> of Gateway Rehabilitation Center

About the Title of this Book

Returning to Joy is an effort to help Torah-observant Jews who find themselves in a state of clinical depression. Torah Jewry is a population that I am intimately familiar with, both personally and professionally. I have had some measure of success in helping people find their way out of depression. In addition, I have been privileged to study under some of the best clinicians and scientists in the area of depression. My hope is to pass what I have learned on to you.

Mitzvah observance has lifted and guided me beyond measure. *Ashreinu mah tov chelkeinu* — how fortunate we are and how good is our lot. At the age of nineteen, however, while studying in yeshivah, I could hardly think about joy or anything beyond keeping my head above water. I was absolutely miserable. My rebbe at the time, as well as my dear *chavrusa*, encouraged me to seek professional help. I am grateful to the *Ribbono shel Olam* that I listened. I am even more grateful that I had the opportunity to work and learn from a wonderful psychotherapist.

While in treatment for my depression, which actually started much earlier in my life, I began the habit of reciting *Tehillim*. Like the countless Jews who have found the sweet words of David HaMelech a balm for an aching soul, I turned to *Tehillim* for help and hope. And it was in Chapter 142 that I found the most exquisite description of depression: "Release my soul from the trap ...in order that the righteous shall use me as a crown to adorn themselves." Depression indeed was a trap. The more I tried to exit it, the more and more tangled I became.

As we chipped away at my depression, that verse stayed with me. The metaphor of being trapped meant that there was a time before Dovid HaMelech was snared. In other words, there was a time when he wasn't depressed. This revelation bothered me. For the life of me I couldn't think of any time when I wasn't depressed. It was then that I came to the jarring realization that as a Jew I had a sacred birthright to joy. It was a place that I could always return to, even if I had never been there before.

It is therefore fitting that a book devoted to helping my brothers and sisters escape from depression be named *Returning to Joy*. My prayer is that you will find in this volume the encouragement and tools that you need to beat your depression. Most importantly, may it be an instrument in finding the joy in life that is your birthright.

Acknowledgments

Having a book published is an exciting event. So many people have made direct and indirect contributions to the volume that you now hold in your hands. I would like to focus on a few of them so that others can learn from these true heroes.

My wife, Beth Mark, has been the most patient and kindest and smartest wife that any husband could ever be married to. She is an example of love and kindness in action.

Our beautiful children (*bli ayin hara*) have made all of the work on this book worth it. Their joy and zest for life is an inspiration to me. May Hashem guide Beth and me in helping these beautiful *neshamos* reach their potential as *b'nei Torah* and sources of *nachas* to *am Yisrael*.

Any book is a journey. The journey of *Returning to Joy* predates the actual writing of the text. It begins with my family, the Mark family of Stamford, Connecticut. My beloved parents, Dr. Julian and Rebecca Mark, have always encouraged me to explore the world and spread my wings. Their zest and kindness has been and always will be an inspiration. My siblings, Susan, Stephanie,

Andrew, and Jane, and their spouses and children have always rooted me on as I followed my path.

My wonderful in-laws, Mr. Bert and Alice Sirote, have loved me as a son. They have been a beacon of warmth and inspiration to Beth and me. May they have much *nachas* from their children and grandchildren.

The wisdom of many of the greatest minds of *Yiddishkeit* and contemporary psychology have shaped the approaches described in *Returning to Joy*. I am immensely fortunate to have studied with *talmidim* of HaRav Yosef Dov Soloveitchik, z"l, who so gently yet powerfully articulated a profoundly positive view of man. Rav Yehuda Parnes, *shlita*, Rav Zvi Schachter, *shlita*, and Rav Dovid Miller, *shlita*, remain role models to this day. They speak with the eloquence of action about what it means to be a true halachic man. May they continue to have much success in the spreading of Torah.

My mentors in the field of psychotherapy are numerous. Chief among them is Dr. Chaim Kranzler, M.D. In the years since our work together I have learned so much from his example as a healer and a *ben Torah*. Rabbi Dr. Abraham Twerski, M.D., who has graced *Returning to Joy* with its beautiful preface, is a role model and teacher to all of us through his writings. Dr. Corey Newman, Ph.D., my supervisor at the Beck Institute for Cognitive Therapy in Philadelphia, has generously given of his time, expertise, and energy to help me use the techniques of cognitive therapy to help thousands of patients.

The staff of Targum Press has been wonderful from the get go. Rabbi Dombey and Miriam Zakon have be-

Acknowledgments

lieved in this project from the moment I proposed it. My editor, Chaya Baila Gavant, has patiently worked with me. Her care and craftsmanship are evident in the book that you now hold.

My gratitude would be incomplete without acknowledgment to the *Ribbono shel Olam*. You have made me an instrument for healing. It is my hope and prayer that my efforts will bear fruit in accordance with Your will. May there come a time soon in our days when books of joy will replace books about depression.

Introduction

Why Another Book about Such a Depressing Topic?

> So I hated life, for I was depressed by all that goes under the sun, because everything is futile and a confusion of the spirit.
>
> *(Koheles* 2:17)

With all of the excellent books for depressed people, what does this book offer that others don't? Fair question. *Returning to Joy* is intended for Torah-observant Jews, an audience that only recently has begun to receive the specialized depression treatment accommodations that it deserves and requires. In some ways this book integrates the excellent material available in such works as *Mind Over Mood* by Dennis Greenberger and Christine Padesky (The Guilford Press, 1995) and *Feeling Good: The New Mood Therapy* by David Burns (Morrow, William & Co, 1999). In many crucial ways, however, this book is directed toward the unique needs, sensitivities, and strengths of Torah-observant Jews.

Why Another Book about Such a Depressing Topic?

As a professional who has helped hundreds of Torah-observant Jews free themselves from the grips of depression, I have long believed that a self-care book presenting balanced information and tried-and-true techniques was needed for our community. Much of the available material inaccurately overemphasizes the biological dimensions of depression and offers few effective techniques for managing the devastating symptoms that have no connection to any of the biological dimensions of clinical depression. Other self-care materials take positions that are dismissive of the biologically based treatments such as antidepressant medications and electroconvulsive therapy which have helped many people.

Returning to Joy is therefore intended to fill a gap in the resources that members of the Torah-observant community need to achieve their potential. It brings together all of the latest available scientific data and research-based methods for the alleviation of depression. In addition, it is designed to respect the sensitivities of Torah-observant Jewry and to utilize the unique strengths that members of our community possess.

The Unique Strengths and Sensitivities of Observant Jews

> Hashem desired to purify Israel; therefore He gave them many mitzvos.
> (*Makos* 23b)

As a way of life, Torah Judaism is a comprehensive blueprint for human health, fulfillment, and happiness. Who can better instruct us on how to live than our Creator? And it is within this instruction manual that we find the most potent antidotes to the conditions discussed in this book. We are fortunate to possess this system and to be charged with showing others how to live.

Because of our allegiance to the Torah way of life, members of our community may dismiss much of the useful secular literature that can help free us of depression. In fact, some of this material reflects values that are at odds with those values that we hold dear. These books occasionally portray male/female relationships, social and family relationships, or attitudes to authority in ways that are unacceptable to Torah-observant Jews. Many of us therefore refuse to use these self-care manuals and media. *Returning to Joy* is respectful of these sensitivities in its approach.

Depression is not only a disorder of the individual. It involves the family and the community. The culture of Torah-observant Jews celebrates the family and community. While the rest of the world is fragmenting into a chaos of self-absorbed individualism, the Torah-observant community stands apart as a warm, embracing shelter. This is one of our greatest strengths. It is this sense of community that is so vital to freedom from depression. The strategies and philosophy espoused in *Returning to Joy* make use of this strength.

The Unique Learning Needs of the Depressed Person

Depression affects the way we learn. When depressed, concentrating becomes an impossible task. It's hard to read and remember. *Returning to Joy* is designed with these weaknesses in mind. Clear writing, brief sec-

Why Another Book about Such a Depressing Topic?

tions, and easy-to-perform exercises make it an extremely helpful text for the depressed person.

The Latest Science on Depression

In recent years the popular press has highlighted the biological aspects of depression. This had made it easier for sufferers to seek help. Billions of dollars have been spent researching and treating depression as a purely biochemical disease.

Unfortunately, in our haste to see depression in this biological light, we have disregarded the significant evidence that many depressions are not simply biological. We now know that there are significant psychological risk factors for depression. When psychological parts of depression are disregarded, treatment is often doomed to fail or to be incomplete. Once medication is stopped, relapses of depression are common. More than half of people using antidepressants do not experience relief. *Returning to Joy* integrates the latest scientific research such as the effects of diet and exercise on mood regulation in its strategies and philosophy.

The Structure of This Book

Returning to Joy is a practical manual for breaking the grip of depression. It contains information and many strategies that have helped many people. *Returning to Joy* begins with a discussion of the raging epidemic of depression. This section has been included in order to reassure both the depressed person and others that he or she is not alone. A balanced discussion about causes of depression is presented.

The bulk of *Returning to Joy* is devoted to relieving

your depression. In order to plan your recovery process, a depression assessment section is included. This section will help you prioritize the chapters and strategies that you want to work on first.

The strategies are grouped around the symptoms of Major Depressive Disorder spelled out in the *Diagnostic and Statistical Manual* of the American Psychiatric Association, 4th edition. Each strategy is designed to be used with a minimum of effort. Since this manual is intended for Torah-observant Jews, *Returning to Joy* indicates sources from classical Jewish texts that validate these strategies.

Returning to Joy and Psychotherapy

> When sick, Rav Yisrael Salanter traveled to Halberstadt. He was seen in his room standing before an open German book doing exercise according to the rules of the book, exactly as his doctor ordered.
> (Rabbi C. E. Zaitchik, *Sparks of Mussar*, p. 55)

In 1994 the United States Department of Health and Human Services convened a prestigious panel of experts. Their job was to determine the standard of treatment for depression. The panel sifted through thousands of scientific studies to determine the best way to help depressed people. Their verdict was a resounding recommendation that patients receive medication and a specialized type of psychotherapy, namely cognitive therapy.

In my experience as mental health professional I have witnessed the wisdom of this recommendation

Why Another Book about Such a Depressing Topic?

proved hundreds of times. *Returning to Joy* is intended to be used in addition to medication and effective psychotherapy. You will be surprised how fast you find your life returns to normal by combining medication, cognitive therapy, and the self-care strategies contained in *Returning to Joy*.

Of course, there are many readers who for many reasons are not receiving effective psychotherapy. The strategies will still be highly effective. Without the support and encouragement of a caring professional, you will have to find ways to stay with the program advocated in *Returning to Joy*. This support and encouragement can come from a family member, a friend, a rebbe, a physician, a support group or any other caring individual.

The Cases and Vignettes in *Returning to Joy*

Privacy is one of the core foundations of helpful psychotherapy. Without the rock-solid trust that a mental health professional will keep everything about treatment in the strictest confidence, patients would simply not open up. Therefore, when reading the vignettes or cases described in *Returning to Joy* please bear in mind that these inspirational stories have no connection to real people. Nevertheless, they are loosely based on the struggles of actual patients who have consulted either with the author or with colleagues. Their inclusion in *Returning to Joy* adds an important dimension: that real people, just like you and I, can beat even the most severe forms of clinical depression.

How to Get the Most Out of This Book

1. Practice

> Bar Hei-Hei said to Hillel: He that reviews his studies a hundred times is not to be compared with he who reviews them a hundred and one times.
>
> (*Chagigah* 9b)

In the second section, "Combating Your Depression," you will learn strategies for managing your mood. The scientifically validated road out of depression lies in the use of skills that affect your brain chemistry and the way that you think. When practicing the skills described in *Returning to Joy* you will find yourself gaining strength. The more that you practice, the more you will be surprised by how good you feel.

2. Make Your Recovery Your Priority

> If I am not for myself, who shall be for me?
>
> (*Avos* 1:14)

Depressed people, like everybody else, live in a world filled with competing demands. Work, family, social obligations, even mitzvos are constantly vying for attention. The depressed person, however, has a particularly difficult time deciding which responsibility comes first. It is not hard to imagine what the inability to manage these conflicts does to one's self-confidence and psyche.

By making recovery the priority, you will find that you can quickly get back on your feet. There are some responsibilities that you will not want to suspend while recovering your joy. Basic mitzvah observance and hy-

Why Another Book about Such a Depressing Topic?

giene are examples that come to mind. But many others can be suspended so that you can devote yourself to the task at hand. Make sure that you make time every day for a month to read this book and to practice the strategies. The investment in time is well worth it.

This is not a license to take a destructive self-indulgent attitude. An insensitive disregard to the feelings and legitimate rights of those around you will lead to deeper self-criticism and despair. Instead, consider striking a balance between self-nurturance and responsibility to others that accommodates your need to spend time caring for your body and soul. A patient once said that she was able to make peace with self-nurturance by realizing that by living with more balance she was setting a positive example for others.

3. Read a Few Pages at a Time

> He who attempts to grasp too much will not retain it. He who grasps a small amount will retain it.
>
> (*Sukkah* 5a)

This book is packed with useful tips. Reading it quickly, however, will sabotage your ability to benefit from the information. By reading a few pages at a time and implementing the information into day, you will find success coming more easily.

4. Go Easy on Yourself

> It is irrelevant if one makes a great sacrifice or a meager sacrifice.
>
> (*Berachos* 5b)

Approach your recovery and the use of this manual

with gentleness. Berating yourself for missing a day of practice or some other infraction will cause greater feelings of self-loathing. Celebrate the fact that you are performing a number of mitzvos by practicing these strategies.

5. Use the Strategies

In my experience as a mental health professional I have seen firsthand how these strategies have helped even the most depressed adults. I have also seen wonderful people linger in their depression far longer than they needed to because they didn't deploy these strategies. It is understandable that you will feel some initial reluctance to keep a daily mood chart or practice guided imagery every day or rewrite your goals every day. This reluctance will depart as soon as you find that these and all of the other strategies are relieving your depression. The only way, however, to get the benefit is to actually use them.

Depression is treatable and beatable. You have the tools in your hands to recover your life from depression. Use these tools, and with your faith in yourself and in the *Ribbono shel Olam,* you will find yourself emerging from the trap of depression.

Learning about Depression

Chapter 1

First Things First: Are You Depressed?

You may be confused about whether you are depressed or not. Is there a difference between sadness and depression? What makes depression any different than the episodes of mental funk that people go through from time to time?

Depression is anything but normal. Regular, run-of-the-mill sadness doesn't prevent you from effectively living your life. Regular sadness doesn't prevent you from getting out of bed or from caring for your body. Sadness comes and goes; depressions linger and get worse. When you are sad and down, you can reach out to others for help. You can do things that lift your spirits. When you are depressed, you can do nothing to free yourself from the pain that binds you.

Review the common symptoms of clinical depression. These are the symptoms of depression listed by the *Diagnostic and Statistical Manual* of the American Psychiatric Association:

- A persistent sad and depressed mood

- Loss of interest or pleasure in hobbies and activities that were once enjoyed
- Loss of appetite and significant weight loss or overeating and weight gain
- Insomnia, early-morning awakening, or oversleeping
- Increased or decreased energy
- Fatigue or feeling "slowed down"
- Difficulty concentrating, remembering, or making decisions
- Feelings of worthlessness and guilt
- Indecisiveness and inability to think or concentrate
- Restlessness or irritability
- Thoughts of death or suicide; or suicide attempts

Contrary to the belief of many, depression and the above symptoms are not a natural emotional state. Joy is an experience that many, many people experience most of their lives. Feelings of depression need not be our regular state of affairs. You too can learn to live joyously. The information in this book will help you get started on that path.

A Depression Self-Test

If you are still unsure as to whether you are depressed, take the following self-test. Circle the statement in each category that is the most right for you. If you are unsure of which statement to choose, select the one with the higher number.

First Things First: Are You Depressed?

Sadness	I do not feel sad.	0
	I feel sad much of the time.	1
	I am sad all the time.	2
	I am so sad or unhappy that I cannot stand it.	3
Loss of interest	I have not lost interest in other people or activities.	0
	I have less interest in other people or things than before.	1
	I have lost most of my interest in other people or things.	2
	It's hard to get interested in anything.	3
Sleep	I sleep well almost every night.	0
	I have trouble falling asleep more than once a week.	1
	I wake up an hour or two before I need to and cannot go back to sleep most nights.	2
	I have difficulty falling asleep and I wake up before I need to most nights.	
Hope and despair	I am not discouraged about my future.	0
	I feel more discouraged about my future than I used to be.	1
	I do not expect things to work out for me.	2
	I feel my future is hopeless and will only get worse.	3

Past failure	I do not feel like a failure.	0
	I have failed more than I should have.	1
	As I look back, I see a lot of failures.	2
	I feel I am a total failure as a person.	3
Appetite	I eat as much as I always do.	0
	I occasionally don't have an appetite.	1
	I frequently avoid eating regular meals.	2
	Others have commented on my weight loss.	3
Self-criticism	I don't criticize or blame myself more than usual.	0
	I am more critical of myself than I used to be.	1
	I criticize myself for all my faults.	2
	I blame myself for everything bad that happens.	3
Suicidal thoughts or wishes	I don't have any thoughts of killing myself.	0
	I have thoughts of killing myself, but I would not carry them out.	1
	I would like to kill myself.	2
	I would kill myself if I had the chance.	3
Anger	I feel relaxed and pleased with life.	0
	I frequently become irritated with myself or others.	1
	I often yell at others or myself.	2
	I feel that I have no control over my anger.	3

First Things First: Are You Depressed?

Shame	I am pleased with myself and my accomplishments.	0
	I see myself as filled with mistakes and without significant accomplishment.	1
	When I am with others I feel embarrassed.	2
	I am totally ashamed of myself.	3
Energy	I have adequate energy and drive to accomplish whatever I want or need to do.	0
	It takes me some time to get moving in order to accomplish those things that I want to accomplish.	1
	It takes me some time to get moving in order to accomplish those tasks that I view as necessities.	2
	Even accomplishing the necessities of life is difficult for me.	3
Memory and concentration	I have no trouble recalling information or concentrating.	0
	I have found recalling information and concentrating becoming increasingly difficult.	1
	I feel that my recall and concentration has significantly gotten in the way of my life.	2
	I find that recalling or concentration is impossible.	3

After completing the questionnaire, add up the numbers. If your score was between 0-4, then you have minimal symptoms of depression. A score of 5-8 means that you have a mild depression. A score of 9-11 reflects a moderate depression. 12 or more means that you have severe depression.

Sadness	Chapter 4: Tackling Your Persistently Depressed Mood
Loss of interest	Chapter 7: Tackling Hopelessness and Pessimism
Sleep	Chapter 5: Tackling Sleep Problems
Hope and despair	Chapter 7: Tackling Hopelessness and Pessimism
Past failure	Chapter 10: Tackling Worthlesness and Guilt
Appetite	Chapter 6: Tackling Appetite Disturbances
Self-criticism	Chapter 10: Tackling Worthlessness and Guilt
Suicidal thoughts or wishes	Chapter 11: Tackling Thoughts of Death and Suicide
Anger	Chapter 12: Irritability and Anger
Shame	Chapter 13: Shame, Modesty, and Self-esteem
Energy	Chapter 8: Tackling Increased or Decreased Energy
Memory and concentration	Chapter 9: Tackling Problems with Concentration, Memory, and Racing Thoughts

First Things First: Are You Depressed?

Planning Your Recovery

The results of this self-test can help you plan your recovery. Use the data from this test to determine where you want to focus in your self-care program. The chapters of *Returning to Joy* are arranged so that you can easily locate the strategies to relieve the symptoms of your depression.

It makes the most sense to begin by alleviating the most severe symptoms. Select the chapter that focuses on your symptoms. You will find loads of strategies that can help you find relief now.

Chapter 2
The Raging Epidemic of Depression

Depression is truly an epidemic. It directly affects millions of people of all industrialized nations. A recent World Health Organization report states that 450 million people are clinically depressed. In the 2001 report of the Surgeon General, depression was the fastest-growing health problem facing American adults. According to the American Psychiatric Association, three people in ten are clinically depressed. Unfortunately, only a small percentage seeks treatment.

A Brief History of the Epidemic

Since the 1950s, epidemiologists, scientists who study the how diseases affect groups of people, have detected an increase in depression among adults. Study after study of many different population groups indicates that we are getting more and more depressed.

Researchers have not been able to determine a single

clear cause for this spread of depression. They have suggested that there have been a number of significant societal changes that make individuals more vulnerable to depression. Some of these causes are increasing social isolation, breakdown of family relationships, advancing technology (especially television), and decreased physical activity.

Depression and the Observant Community

There is of yet no statistical indication that the epidemic of depression among the general population is also affecting the observant Torah community. On the other hand, the fact that more and more mental health clinics devoted to treating our community have opened up seems to indicate that more of us are seeking treatment. Furthermore, the societal trends suspected to be some of the causes of the depression epidemic in the general population are no stranger to our community. The variety of self-help and professional organizations composed of Torah-observant Jews popping up is further evidence that depression is making inroads into the Torah world.

The Costs of Untreated Depression in Our Community

> To the wise the way of life leads upward, that he may depart from Sheol beneath.
>
> (*Mishlei* 15:24)
>
> Man was created by himself to teach you that whoever causes the loss of one Jew is causing the loss of an entire universe.
>
> (*Sanhedrin* 4:5)

Social scientists tell us that the cost of depression in the United States exceeds seventy billion dollars per year. This number includes missed days of work, unemployment, or poor productivity. When the secondary costs of depression, such as the cost of treating medical illnesses related to depression, family violence, addictions, and poor academic performance, are factored in, the cost becomes truly astronomical.

In the Torah view, however, loss of money is only the beginning of evaluating the cost of any condition. Certainly the most devastating price of depression is the loss of life through suicide. In recent years a rise in this extreme symptom of depression has become increasingly familiar to us. Successful and talented *b'nei Torah*, wonderful mothers, and blossoming young people have taken this horrible route.

Lying in between the economic costs of depression and suicide are lives that fail to fully blossom. So many members of our community live their lives in a state of low grade agony. Consider the impact that depression has on one's ability to parent a child (much less a large family), or to learn, or to teach, and to serve God as we all strive to do. Now multiply this impact by the thousands of our brothers and sisters who also suffer with depression and the children and spouses who are the secondary victims. The cost of depression to the Torah-observant community is incalculable.

The Good News

We are the children of Avraham, who believed that God can send His Divine Light into an individual's heart, even if the individual is unworthy of that Light.

(Rav Tzadok HaKohen of Lublin)

There is much good news, however, to acknowledge. Treatment for depression is becoming more effective. This is occurring on several different fronts. As scientists better understand the different kinds of depression, biological treatments are emerging to more accurately target the individual manifestations of depression.

In addition, the pendulum toward viewing depression as strictly a biological disease is beginning to move back toward the more logical middle road. There is greater availability of effective psychotherapy for depression. The professional community is more willing than ever to treat depression as much more complex than simply a chemical imbalance or psychological hang-ups taken too far.

The prevention of depression is becoming a priority. Yes, there are ways to prevent depression which are much more effective than treatment after the fact. Emotional intelligence management training is being implemented in public schools and the initial results indicate that depression can be headed off at the pass.

In the Torah-observant community, there is greater willingness to learn about depression. More and more of us are seeking treatment before the depression rages out of control. Help lines, books, lectures, and clinics are making it easier for everyone to get help.

We are blessed to live in a community that has much strength. Not so long ago, the Torah-observant community banded together to stamp out Tay Sachs disease.

Dor Yeshorim was born and we are now reaping the benefits of a decrease in this devastating disease. Bone marrow match drives are community wide. The Torah-observant community is envied for its ability to respond to the pressing needs of others. Hopefully, this superhuman energy and cohesiveness can be harnessed to take on and conquer depression in our midst.

Chapter 3

The Causes of Depression

Depression is a human condition whose causes have long been the focus of a spirited debate. At present the two most dominant hypotheses focus on either brain biology or psychological causes. Most likely the true answer lies somewhere in between. Depression is a highly individual disorder, and it is logical that its causes are individual as well.

Why It Is Important to Know the Causes of Depression

Knowing why someone gets depressed is important. It helps the sufferer, his or her family or friends, and professionals determine what should be done to alleviate the symptoms. When the cause of depression is known, the sufferer can avoid future depressions by avoiding the cause. He or she can also implement strategies to lessen the negative effects of the causes on his or her thinking and mood.

In the last twenty years, the search for a biological

cause of depression has served an additional purpose. Identifying some of the possible biological aspects of depression has given many millions of people permission to speak openly of their depression and to get help for it. Many cultural values conspire to make it socially acceptable to speak of being depressed because of brain physiology. The fact that many members of the Torah-observant community now seek treatment for depression because our community sees it as a biologically based disease is a positive consequence of this phenomenon.

The Biological Causes of Depression

The most well known biological hypothesis focuses on serotonin. The millions of cells throughout the body are in constant contact with each other. The method of connection is through the secretion and absorption of hundreds of different types of neurotransmitters. A breakdown in this delicate communication process will cause havoc in the affected organs.

In the case of depression, the communication between the brain cells in the region of the brain responsible for mood regulation and decision-making is disrupted. This disruption in communication is believed to be caused by the failure of several neurotransmitters, serotonin being the most well known of them, to adequately perform its function. Other neurotransmitters that are suspected to play a role in depression are dopamine, noradrenaline, and norepinephrine.

Evidence for the biological view of depression is easy to find. Identical twins separated at birth and reared apart had a similar incidence of depression. This

The Causes of Depression

finding strongly suggests that there is a genetically based, biological predisposition to depression. Advanced brain imaging techniques clearly show that the brains of depressed people operate differently than the brains of those who are not depressed.

Antidepressant medications are believed to fix the hypothesized neurotransmitter glitches. Most of these medications focus on changing how serotonin is used in the parts of the brain most involved in depression. Other medications target the other neurotransmitters as well. (See appendix B for a list of antidepressant medications.)

The Psychological Causes of Depression

Of the many psychological explanations for depression, only the cognitive model has shown enduring validity. The cognitive model states that the way the depressed person thinks causes depression. A lifelong style of thinking in a depression-prone manner makes one's mind vulnerable to the helplessness of depression.

What is a depression-prone style of thinking? How does such thinking cause depression? The two most significant proponents of the cognitive model of depression, Martin Seligman and Aaron Beck, speak of cognitive biases. Through their study of hundreds of thousands of people, their research over the last thirty years has shown that the depression-prone person relates to him or herself, his or her environment, and his or her future in a habitual, self-destructive mix of pessimism, passivity, and all-or-nothing thinking.

Prior to a depression, depression-prone people tend

to ascribe exaggerated control of their feelings to people and events outside of themselves. Depression-prone people have difficulty distinguishing between feelings and facts. Feelings about themselves, events, and others are given much greater value than cold, hard facts. When it comes to self-evaluation they tend to be overly self-critical.

At first glance, readers may react to the cognitive model with legitimate objections. *But everyone thinks that way!* When a friend or a spouse says something insulting, everyone feels angry. To not feel hurt is to not be human. Are we all supposed to be robots?

Yes, feelings make us gloriously human. Even cognitive therapists get their feelings hurt. And we wouldn't want it to be any other way. The everyday hurts that we all encounter are like jabs to our stomach. When hit in the stomach, everyone doubles over. The depression-prone person, however, has reduced ability to right himself. While the depression-resilient person has dusted himself off and resumed his life with an intact sense of self, the depression-prone person lingers in pain. He ruminates over the wound, and even when he recovers the painful experience contributes to a deeper pessimistic belief in himself and in his future. This pessimism leads to an emotionally protective stance that prevents him from taking action and risk in his environment. Social activity begins to slow down. Once social contact declines, self-esteem begins to deteriorate, and the depression-prone person has entered the final trajectory into depression.

The Causes of Depression

Physical Inactivity and Diet

Theories about brain physiology and psychology are the twin pillars of understanding the causes of depression. Nevertheless, some findings about the effects of physical inactivity and diet on mood have emerged in recent years. The implications of these findings are of significant relevance and must be included in the discussion of causes of depression.

Here is a smattering of the gathering data.

- Depressed people who engaged in light exercise for thirty minutes four times per week went into remission within a month. They remained depression free for a year even when they stopped exercising.

- Finnish women who consumed one serving of fish per week were fifty times more likely to be depression free than those who did not.

As research about depression progresses, it is quite likely that our global decrease in physical activity and poor diet will be identified as key factors in the epidemic of depression.

So What Is the Bottom Line?

Depression is a complex disorder. Since depression manifests itself differently in each of us, it seems reasonable to assume that there is no single cause for depression. In fact, there is ample evidence to make a case for both sides. Changes in brain function in people taking antidepressant medications supports the biological viewpoint. The scientific and medical literature provides a solid range of cure rates when antidepressant medication is used.

On the other hand, similar changes can be detected in people receiving cognitive therapy. This obscures whether the biological disruption is the cause or the effect of the psychological symptoms. The most accurate answer, therefore, is that it is a little of both.

Some cases of depression are much more biological than psychological. There are many women who do not possess any of the psychological risks factors who develop postpartum depression. There are many individuals who are free of these risk factors but become extremely depressed following coronary bypass surgery or when taking certain types of medications for various physical ailments. These are examples of clearly biologically based depressions where biologically based treatment is the way to go.

Parallel to this are those of us who clearly have psychologically based depressions. In such cases, psychological treatment that emphasizes changing destructive ways of thinking and learning mood management skills would be the best choice.

The regrettable situation is that many depression sufferers often get the wrong treatments. Women with postpartum depression are offered psychological treatment when in fact they should often start with antidepressant medication under the supervision of a gynecologist. Men who have long-standing habits of passivity and black-and-white thinking are given medication without any intervention for their thinking habits. Or they may be offered forms of psychotherapy that have been proven over and over again to be of no use in the treatment of depression. Despite the ample professional and lay literature that supports a flexible approach to treatment, many clinicians and lay people are in the dark about what helps and what doesn't.

An Antidepressant Lifestyle: The Sensible Approach for Torah-Observant Jews

When it comes to treatment, scientific study after study supports a multifaceted approach. For those of us who want to feel better and stay better, the combination of antidepressant medication and psychotherapy is the way to go. In addition to medication and therapy, physical exercise, diet, and the strategies included in this book are the components to the best antidote to depression and the prevention to future episodes.

Combating Your Depression

Chapter 4

Tackling Your Persistently Depressed Mood

Depression distorts everything. There is not one aspect of your daily existence that is unaffected by depression. Thinking, feeling, social relationships, eating, and sleeping are burdensome. Even the passage of time seems to become distorted. The strategies that follow will help you regain your strength and focus.

Because of depression's impact on your thinking, it is vital that you reach out to others for help. Without the assistance of competent and compassionate professionals, you will continue to languish in your depressed mood. This section will show you how to find the mental health professional who is right for you. You will also learn how to get the most out of that valuable relationship.

Ultimately, you are responsible for the lifting of your mood. The mental health professional you choose to work with you and the self-care strategies in this book can show you the way out of your depressed mood. This section contains some of the basic mood regulation skills that can restore your emotional freedom. Their usefulness increases each time that you use them. They will help you start taking back your mood.

Working with a Mental Health Professional

A prisoner cannot free himself from a prison.
(*Berachos* 5b)

Despite whatever reluctance you may have about meeting with a mental health professional, now is the time to go. Treatment is the surest way out of depression and back into life. Some problems in life can be solved by reading a book or watching a video. Depression is not that kind of problem. Because of depression's distorting effect on the way that you think and feel, you will find it enormously difficult to improve your life on your own. The right therapist will help you feel better faster and more completely than you could ever hope to on your own.

How does a therapist do this? A competent therapist will evaluate your present symptoms and your history. He or she will examine the factors that contribute to your present difficulties and then recommend steps that you can take to feel better. The therapist will guide you and cheer you on as you take the steps out of depression and back into life.

Consider the words of Freeda, thirty-nine, wife, and mother of six:

> *My depression probably started right after shivah ended when my mother died. But it really got bad during the following winter. After stalling for a month I fi-*

nally contacted a clinical social worker who was well respected in our community. I stalled because I thought that I would bounce back from feeling so low. And the fact is that there were times when I actually felt okay. But the lows were something I had never experienced before. The craziest thoughts came into my head and I worked so hard to get them out. It took a lot out of me.

The social worker helped me talk about how I was feeling. The more I talked about the crazy feelings in her office, the less I thought about them during the rest of the week. But we didn't only talk; she guided me on how to improve my mood. My fear of others finding out turned out to be ridiculous. And considering how miserable I was, having others know my business should have been the last thing I should have worried about.

Therapy helped a lot. Within a couple of weeks I was getting through the day without crying jags. My concentration at work and at home also got better almost right away.

Strategy 1: Choose the Right Mental Health Professional

> He who follows after righteousness and kindness finds life, righteousness, and honor.
>
> (*Mishlei* 21:21)

Psychotherapy is provided by many different types of professionals. Social workers, psychologists, psychiatrists, family therapists, nurses, and many *rabbanim* all provide psychotherapy. The most common psychotherapists are social workers, psychologists, and psychiatrists. Social workers usually have a minimum of a master's and two-year internship. In the United States, most mental health services are provided by social workers. Social workers specialize in different styles of psychotherapy, such as psychoanalysis or cognitive therapy. They also tend to look at depression as involving not only your mind but also your family relationships and work.

Psychiatrists are medical doctors who specialized in the diagnosis and treatment of psychiatric disorders. They have completed four years of medical school and then completed a four-year residency in adult psychiatry. Some psychiatrists have advanced training in different types of psychotherapy. Of all the professionals who offer psychotherapy, they are the only ones who can prescribe medications.

Psychologists have either a master's or a doctorate in different areas of psychology. They are also required to have several years of different internships. Unlike social workers and psychiatrists, psychologists are specially trained in psychological testing and assessment. Many psychologists have advanced training in the treatment of different psychological disorders.

Selecting the right professional is a crucial step. The decision of who to work with should be done with research and deliberation. It is ironic and unfortunate that in a depressed state, when most of us have great difficulty making even the simplest of decisions, we have to choose who we will work with to make our lives better. For this reason, word of mouth is often the best way to find a mental health professional. Ask a confidante or a physician if he or she knows of someone. Networking with others is usually the best way to get the right person the first time.

Tackling Your Persistently Depressed Mood

Nevertheless, many of us don't have a friend whose guidance we can seek. It may be awkward to disclose to an acquaintance that you are depressed and are looking for a therapist. In such situations, the next best place is to start with a local mental health agency. Such services can be found under "hospitals" or "counseling" in most phone books. Many mental health centers advertise in newspapers and magazines as well. Some people may have insurance plans that offer very efficient and competent mental health services. You can find out more by contacting your insurance company.

There are two essential qualities to look for in a mental health professional. These are competence and compassion. Competence is the product of training and experience. When "shopping" for a therapist you have every right to ask about where he or she received their training to provide psychotherapy services. You should also ask about experience in the field. You can also certainly ask questions about their approach to helping people with depression.

The most scientifically valid approach is cognitive behavior therapy. This type of treatment focuses on changing the ways of thinking that cause your depression. A cognitive therapist will aggressively treat your present symptoms.

The second quality, compassion, is harder to evaluate. Look for someone whom you feel comfortable with. You are going to open up to this person. Do you feel that you can trust them? Because therapy often involves making changes that you will improve your life, do you feel that the therapist will be supportive? In a state of depression you may be less capable of making such judgments about anybody. Nevertheless, it is important that you try to pay attention to the relationship dimension of therapy.

Consider the words of Yona, twenty-eight, husband, father of three, and attorney:

> *My wife and sister kept on pushing me to seek professional help. In order to save money I decided to use one of the clinical psychologists that were on my insurance plan. It took me two sessions to figure out that this was not going to work. The psychologist seemed like he was nervous and unfocused. Maybe I just couldn't relate to him. I contacted the insurance company and they let me switch to another psychologist. He was much better. He focused on the here and now and I quickly got the feeling that he knew what he was doing. He did, and I got better.*

Strategy 2: Prepare for Treatment

You want freedom from depression. You want to resume finding satisfaction in life. The competent and compassionate assistance of a mental health professional can get you there. How long the process takes and how much it costs depends on many factors. Like all things in life, success has much to do with how much you put into treatment. Preparing for treatment can help you get where you want to go much faster.

When you meet with a mental health professional for the first time, it is often a good idea to bring a family member or good friend along with you. They can help you find the office. They can help reassure you if you are worried or ambivalent about keeping the appointment. In some cases the professional may want to ask him or her, with your permission, to join in the initial meeting.

Your family member or friend may be able to supply information that you may be unable to.

It is particularly important, especially at the first meeting, to bring a list of medications that you are taking. This list should include vitamins, supplements, homeopathic remedies, and all over-the-counter medications that you regularly use. If you have access to current blood tests, that information can only speed up the therapist's formulation of how best to help you.

Invest some time in writing down your symptoms. When do they get worse and when do they get better? What do you think caused your depression? Are there members of your family who have had depression or other psychiatric illness? Have you gone through any significant life-changing events within the last year? Have you had a major physical illness in the last year? Have you experienced a trauma that is related to your depression? These are a few of the important questions that your mental health professional will want to know at the beginning of treatment.

As treatment progresses, it is still important to prepare for therapy sessions. The more effort that you put into your therapy, the more benefit you will receive. Prior to each session, consider asking yourself the following thought-provoking questions:

1. What problem do I want to work on this week?
2. How have I been feeling this week compared to other weeks?
3. What happened this week that my therapist should know about?
4. What did we cover during the last session?

5. Was there anything that bothered me about last session? Any unfinished business?
6. Is there anything that I am reluctant to tell my therapist?

If you keep a journal or diary, consider taking that to your session. There may be material that you might decide to share with your therapist. A diary or a journal is also a good place to record information from your therapy session that you want to remember.

Consider the words of David, forty-four, husband and father of five, computer analyst:

I began keeping a journal after the second session. It was one of those Mead composition books that I used in high school. I wrote down everything in it. Thoughts, feelings, dreams, wishes, divrei Torah, my budget, to-do lists, everything. I also wrote down things my psychiatrist said that I thought were worth remembering. I would just say in the middle of a session that I wanted to write that down. It's been several years since my depression. I look back at that journal from time to time to see how far I have come, but also to remind me of what I still need to learn. The journal really helped.

Strategy 3: Identify All of Your Symptoms

When we are depressed we are most aware of the most painful parts of the disease. Our deep anguish, however, prevents us from becoming fully aware of other symptoms. These symptoms, such as poor sleep or loss of appetite, in fact often make recovery from depression even more difficult. Because we are mostly unaware of them, we don't take the steps necessary to eliminate them.

Tackling Your Persistently Depressed Mood

The *Diagnostic and Statistical Manual* of the American Psychiatric Association lists the following symptoms of depression. As you study this list, make a note of those symptoms that you experience most intensely and frequently. Ask others, especially your therapist, for help with these symptoms.

- A persistent sad, anxious, or "empty" mood
- Feelings of hopelessness and pessimism
- Feelings of guilt, worthlessness, and helplessness
- Loss of interest or pleasure in hobbies and activities that were once enjoyed
- Decreased energy, fatigue, or feeling "slowed down"
- Difficulty concentrating, remembering, or making decisions
- Insomnia, early-morning awakening, or oversleeping
- Appetite and/or weight loss or overeating and weight gain
- Thoughts of death or suicide; or suicide attempts
- Restlessness or irritability
- Persistent physical symptoms that have not responded to treatment, such as headaches, digestive disorders, and chronic pain

In addition to this list of symptoms, the following questions can help you clarify your other, more subtle symptoms.

- What do I feel?

- What am I thinking?
- How does my body feel?
- What am I doing?

Make sure to share this information with your mental health professional. He or she can offer ways to change or eliminate symptoms.

Strategy 4: Tell Your Mental Health Professional Everything

Opening up to a stranger is difficult. As Torah-observant Jews, we value modesty and privacy. We avoid *lashon hara* and refrain from speaking ill of others, especially our parents and teachers. The Torah demands that we fight the *yetzer hara* at every step. We therefore may be inclined to refuse to discuss matters that we associate with the *yetzer hara*. And this is exactly as it should be.

Because of these rules, however, many patients mistakenly fail to share areas of personal difficulty with their mental health professional. The refusal to discuss areas of pain is self-sabotaging. Depressions thrive on destructive and excessive secrecy. And the distorted use of modesty or the prohibition of *lashon hara* will lead to worse and worse depression.

In order to help patients better understand the importance of opening up about embarrassing matters, I reassure them that everything discussed in our office is private. It will never make its way into shul, the local *beis midrash*, or the local seminary. Unless he or she gives me written permission, I, as a psychotherapist, may not even confirm that they are in treatment. They are assured 100 percent confidentiality.

They are also assured of my unquestioned respect for them. No matter what they have done, they will always be capable of respect in my eyes. Each human being is created in the image of Hashem no matter what. I remind them of the people described in Tanach, the Talmud, and elsewhere whose most private affairs were revealed to all. Yet no one disputes that Yehudah or David HaMelech were among the greatest members of the Jewish people.

With regard to *lashon hara*, patients are told that I am committed to helping them achieve the most respectful relationship that they can. Strict adherence to halachah is the foundation for all healthy and productive relationships. In order to achieve such a relationship we must look at all its relevant parts, both the good and the bad. Similar to draining an infected wound, the negative parts must be drained before the healing can begin.

Modesty issues are addressed in a similar fashion. Therapy is a tool that has an excellent track record for helping people make changes in their lives. If you wish to change what you think about or some behavior pattern that distresses you, then the tools of effective therapy can help you. It does require, however, that you open up about that which you wish to change.

Different mental health professionals may have different ways of responding to your concerns. It is important that you make clear what areas of your life you are willing to discuss and which areas are off limits. No matter what you decide, openness to your therapist is of vital importance to your success.

Attending to Your Physiological Needs

Strategy 1: Consider Using Antidepressant Medications

Depressions distort the way we think and feel. Depressions also involve the way our bodies operate. This is particularly the case with how the brain operates. Without fixing that brain physiology, the resolution of our depression will be needlessly much harder.

One very effective way to fix the disrupted brain is the use of antidepressant medications. These medications have helped millions of people emerge from states of depression. The medications, without changing who we are, help the portions of our brains responsible for our moods and judgment perform their responsibilities more effectively.

Antidepressants don't make us happy. They don't make us think more positively. They certainly don't make our life situations better. Antidepressants do make it easier to think clearly and to do those things that make our lives better and give us joy.

Here is a useful metaphor. Picture yourself in the driver's seat of a car. You are stopped at a red light. The light turns green. In your first effort you must release your foot from the brake. Then you must step on the accelerator and turn the steering wheel as necessary. Simply releasing the brake pedal will not help you move forward. You will still have to depress the accelerator and turn the steering wheel as necessary.

Just like releasing the brakes of your car, antidepressant medications will release much of the physiological stuff that is getting in the way of your life. Once these factors are released, however, you still have to go about living your life in the most effective way possible. Living carelessly by ignoring your spiritual, emotional, social, and physical well-being will undermine all of the progress that medications may help bring about. That is why psychotherapy and all of the work of depression recovery must be combined with the use of medication.

Strategy 2: Take Antidepressant Medication the Right Way

It seems easy to take medication. Many of us have taken some kind of medication for one problem or another. Many people, however, don't use antidepressant medications the way they were intended to be used. The result is that patients don't get the full benefit from the medication.

The most important step in using antidepressant medication is to take it. Even the best medication will be useless if it remains in the pill bottle. If you have qualms about taking medication, then talk them over with your mental health professional. He or she can help you feel more comfortable with this valuable treatment.

The second most important step in benefiting from medications is to take them even when you feel well. The temptation to stop taking your medication is often quite strong. Avoid it especially when you do so without consulting with your mental health professional. Because there is the risk of reoccurrence of depression, continued use of medication protects you from further episodes. Furthermore, abruptly stopping your medications can cause unwanted physical reactions. So if you have decided to discontinue antidepressant medication, do so with the assistance of your mental health professional.

Strategy 3: Maintain a Healthy Diet

> A healthy body is one of the routes to Hashem, since one cannot comprehend Hashem if his body is ill. Therefore, one must avoid those behaviors that undermine the body and follow those habits that restore physical health.
> (Rambam, *Hilchos Dei'os* 4:1)

Food has an enormous influence on your interest in life. When you are well nourished, your brain and body can put forth the energy necessary to find passion and enjoyment in life. When you are poorly nourished, every thought becomes a struggle. The result is deeper and deeper despair. Even if you are taking antidepressant medication and receiving first-rate treatment, a poor diet will undermine your efforts to improve your mood. The importance of a healthful and vitalizing diet for depression recovery cannot be underestimated.

Because depression, particularly extended bouts of depression, disturbs our thinking, changes in diet may seem unrealistic. "I cannot do that" or "I have tried to change my diet and it never works" are among the most common reasons that depressed adults give for avoiding the issue of food. These thoughts, however, are based on the depressed person's distorted way of thinking. Any changes that you decide to take should be small and attainable. You don't even need to commit to eating power-generating foods for the rest of your life. Simply have one power-generating meal.

Nutritional needs are highly individualized. Changes in your diet should be made with the assistance of a qualified dietician. She or he has the knowl-

Tackling Your Persistently Depressed Mood

edge to help you find foods and a food regimen that will support you in your recovery. Dieticians can share strategies that will assist you in making any necessary changes in your diet. Ask your mental health professional for a referral to a dietician that he or she is familiar with. If your therapist is unable, then many hospitals will help you find one.

In addition to what your dietician will teach you about diet, the following is of particular relevance to the depressed adult.

1. There are foods and nutrients that appear to have a potent effect on mood. While the available research is inconclusive, a diet that includes two servings of fish per week has a depression-busting effect. Diets that contain an abundance of simple carbohydrates appear to be correlated with greater depression. *The Brain Chemistry Plan* (Perigee, 2003) and *The Brain Chemistry Diet* (Putnam Publishing Group, 2001) by Dr. Michael Lesser contain more information on what foods to increase and what foods to avoid.

2. Replace artificial, refined, and processed junk foods with healthy foods. Let's face it. Junk foods are called junk foods because they are junk. Junk goes into a trash can, not a human being. When you want a snack, reach for an apple, a banana, yogurt, or pretzels. Choose foods that will make you feel better twenty minutes from now, not just right now.

    This doesn't mean that you should deny yourself treats and candy. It simply means that you avoid relying on snack food as a substitute for

healthy food and regular meals. It also means that you treat your body as the miraculous treasure that it is.
3. Routinize your eating habits. Eat each of your meals at the same time every day. This will help you make sure that you get the proper nutrition. This habit will also help you track how you feel after each meal.
4. Monitor the effects of different foods on your energy levels and mood. People often find that certain foods affect them negatively. Some report that after having pasta or other starches at lunch they feel sleepy and lethargic. Many people believe that monosodium glutamate has negative effects. Ask yourself how you feel after you eat, so that you avoid foods that interfere with your life.
5. Go easy on yourself. When it comes to changing any type of habit, we often take two steps forward, one step backwards. When you succeed in eating healthfully, celebrate yourself. If you slide backwards, go easy on yourself. At least you are trying to improve your diet. Try to learn from your mistake(s) so that you don't slip again.

Develop a Goal-oriented Mind-Set

It may seem ludicrous to think of goals when you are in a deep depression. That's because you are thinking with your depression head. The fact is goals, whether they be large and daunting or small and easy, promote a sense of direction. Goals help us focus on what we can do to make our lives better.

Tackling Your Persistently Depressed Mood

Focusing on the achievement of goals is in fact one of the most important antidepressant strategies that you can utilize. It's a habit that is easy to develop. The best part of this change is that you will immediately feel less depressed just by taking the first steps toward your goals.

In order to do this, expand your horizons. People with long-term depressions usually have great difficulty setting goals. This is due to demoralization that comes with depression. Your horizon is limited to making it through the day.

The antidote to an absence of goals is to expand your horizons. Look around you and try to notice life beyond your depression. You may notice activities that appeal to you. When you can look at life with joy and forgiveness, you see opportunities everywhere.

I often draw a picture of a valley for my patients. I explain that the lower he or she is in the valley of depression, the narrower his or her horizon will appear. Once the patient can see beyond the limits of their narrow horizon, he or she can begin to set more goals.

Look compassionately inside yourself. Identify some goal or achievement that you once aspired to. Is there some aspect of yourself that you would like to improve? Is there some area that you would like to learn about? Perhaps there is a cause that you have always wanted to get involved in.

Set goals in all the areas of your life. These areas include health, social, vocational, financial, enjoyment, spiritual, and emotional. Develop short-term and long-term goals in each area.

Here is a list of examples of goals.

RETURNING TO JOY

AREA	SPECIFIC GOALS
Health	Improve diet; get more exercise; get more sleep; improve hygiene
Social	Become more interested in others; increase generosity; become more trustworthy
Vocation	Get a job; get job training; explore new areas of work
Financial	Create a budget; save money; cut down debt
Enjoyment	Participate in a hobby; read a book; go to the movies
Spiritual	Help others; develop a more spiritual life
Emotional	Manage anger; overcome shyness; cultivate a positive attitude

Now that you have determined your goals, accomplishing them is next. If you have met with failure in the past, then take heart. The following strategies were probably not in your arsenal at the time. By applying the following rules with some optimism and forgiveness, you will find goal achievement within your each.

Strategy 1: Break Down Your Goals

Start with a big goal and then break it down into smaller goals. These smaller goals are short-term and mid-term goals. Each accomplishment of these middle steps brings you closer to the fulfillment of the long-term goal. It may be easier to think of this concept as climbing a flight of stairs. Consider the following diagram:

Tackling Your Persistently Depressed Mood

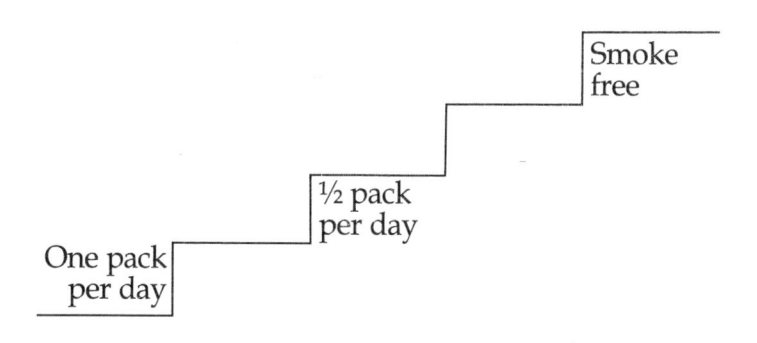

```
                          ┌─────────┐
                          │ Smoke   │
                          │ free    │
                ┌─────────┤
                │ ½ pack  │
                │ per day │
    ┌───────────┤
    │ One pack  │
    │ per day   │
```

By breaking them down into short-term, mid-term, and long-term objectives, you make the process of goal attainment even easier. If you find that accomplishing the component of the goal is beyond your reach, then it is a sign that you still have not broken the goal down into small enough parts.

The following table shows some other examples of how larger goals can be broken down into smaller goals.

Strategy 2: Review Your Goals Regularly

The surge in motivation that we experience when we first think of a goal evaporates like steam on a cold winter day. The only remedy for this is constant review. Reread your goals several times a day. Write them down on a piece of paper, photocopy it, and stick it next to your bathroom mirror, on your refrigerator, next to your bed...everywhere. If others look a bit in askance at you or make light of your efforts, dismiss their comments and attitudes. It is your life and your recovery that we're talking about here.

Strategy 3: Don't Worry about Finishing

Some depressed people avoid setting goals because

AREA	LONG TERM	SHORT TERM	MID TERM
Health	Better diet	Eat single servings of snack food	Consume five cups of water a day
Social	More interest in others	Say hello with a smile to three strangers	Ask a coworker out for coffee
Vocational	Get job training	Get a catalog of upcoming courses at a local community college or technical school	Contact the community college about registering for a course
Finance	Create a budget	Complete a budget form	Follow the budget for one week
Enjoyment	Participate in a hobby	Go to a hobby store and see what suits your interests	Purchase a hobby kit
Emotional	Manage anger	Write down five things that you got angry about today	Rehearse how you could have responded to the trigger without any anger

Tackling Your Persistently Depressed Mood

of the fear that they may not finish the process. The key to sneaking around the negativism of your depression head is to get into the process without worrying about the end result.

Strategy 4: Manage the Fear of Pain

The depressed person is so focused on basic survival that reaching for even the smallest goal may seem too painful. It is understandable to avoid pain. However, the depressed person is even afraid of the fear of pain. When you encounter this fear you retreat backwards into an imaginary cocoon of safety.

The fear of pain, however, is a manifestation of the depression head. Breaking your goals into smaller objectives is the best way to reduce fear of pain. Smaller objectives are less intimidating and easier to tackle. Once you crash through the imaginary wall of fear, you will find greater energy and courage on the other side.

Strategy 5: Get Started Already!!

Depressed people delay starting the process of achieving a goal because they are waiting for something else to happen. "I'll start changing my diet at the end of the month." "I'll open a savings account when I get my next paycheck." There is no guarantee that you will be any more able to get started then, so why wait? Right now (even if it's the middle of the night and it's raining) is a great time to get started on a goal.

Strategy 6: Don't Take No for an Answer

If you set out attaining a goal and meet with failure, it doesn't mean that the goal was wrong. It doesn't mean that you are a failure or unworthy of attaining the goal.

It simply means that you may have to adjust your strategy. You may have to revise your definition of the goal. The "no" that you may be encountering may really be a sign that says "good goal; bad planning."

Strategy 7: Stick with Goal Setters

Depressed people must be selective about whom they associate with. Family members, friends, acquaintances, coworkers, or neighbors who don't set goals for themselves may be cynical or derisive of your efforts at self-improvement. Avoid them. They will only hold you back. Find people who encourage you and who are also trying to improve their lives. Let their positive attitude rub off on you and let your positive attitude rub off on them.

Strategy 8: Don't Confuse "Hard" with "Impossible"

All of us at some time in our lives say to ourselves or to others that some goal is "hard." "Learning how to operate a computer is hard." "Exercising regularly is hard." "Improving my diet is hard." "Putting twenty dollars a month in a savings account is hard." When most of us make statements along these lines, we really mean that a certain goal is impossible to accomplish. That's a false assumption. Anything that we can conceive of doing can be accomplished. History has demonstrated this over and over again. Don't let the fact that something is hard stop you.

Celebrate Your Small Successes

> An effort made below triggers an effort above.
> (*Zohar, Pekudei* 264b)

> Whenever the great *mussar* teacher Rav Nosson Zvi Finkel saw a good deed in a student, he would praise and honor him, speak to him for hours, and sometimes even hug and kiss him. This was especially true when the deed was one of *chessed*, such as doing someone a favor or visiting the sick.
>
> *(Sparks of Mussar*, p. 183)

Depression devastates your interest in life. It robs you of personal power. Depression brings up shame because you see yourself as horribly imperfect. The antidote to shame is through the actions of self-celebration. Self-celebration serves to puncture the negative self-talk and ruminations which occupy your depressed mind. Consider the following ideas regarding self-celebration.

Strategy 1: Celebrate Everything

No matter what, you have something to celebrate. Recovery and healing is made up of tiny little victories over your symptoms. Whether it is refraining from giving into impulse or simply breathing, you are worthy of celebration. Celebrate every thought or action, however seemingly insignificant, that helps you move in the direction of life and healing.

Strategy 2: Look for Things to Celebrate

Actively search for causes for celebration. This is especially important if you are experiencing self-loathing. Self-loathing is baseless. Every human being is a work in progress. Even if you have done something that you regret, you can still change yourself and improve yourself. Self-loathing is in fact a cop-out because it prevents you from taking corrective action. If you are experiencing self-loathing, look for the smallest positive action that you perform and celebrate it. At first you may have to do this through gritted teeth. With sufficient repetition, however, it will become easier.

Consider the words of Tali, mother of six, wife, and teacher:

> *After the birth of Yocheved I developed postpartum depression. I know that postpartum depression is mostly chemical, but I also felt that there was something psychological as well. Having such a wonderful baby is a blessing, but being home all the time cut me off from my social network. My psychiatrist recommended that I focus on accomplishing some goals. I knew that she was right because I do feel better when I accomplish a big job. She encouraged to find little ways to pat myself on the back as I moved in the right direction.*
>
> *About this time, my state teacher's certification was expiring. It was a real hassle to renew it. I needed to complete forms, get letters, have them notarized, copy them, and then submit them. So many details. I made up a list of what needed to be done. There must have been thirty steps! Whenever I completed one step I treated myself to different things — a candy bar, a new music tape, a long bath, or sometimes simply a glow inside of getting closer to my goal. When I got the project done my husband took me out to our favorite restaurant. Since then I always make sure that I have a project to work on and that I take the time to celebrate my efforts.*

Or consider the words of Ephraim, a twenty-three-year-old *yeshivah bachur*.

Tackling Your Persistently Depressed Mood

My therapist and I spent a couple of sessions working on how to rebuild my self-esteem. I decided that setting some learning goals would give me a sense of accomplishment. He helped me come up with a program. Instead of looking at the whole thing and getting depressed and demoralized, I focused on each small step. In order to strengthen my "one step at a time" mind-set, I would take some time to savor each accomplishment. Sometimes I would treat myself to an ice cream bar, and other times to a walk in the park.

Strategy 3: Celebrate in a Concrete Way

It's not enough to say to yourself, "Great job." You must do something. It need not be a big activity. Buy yourself a candy bar, compliment yourself verbally, listen to music for a few minutes, or write the action in your notebook or journal. Concrete celebration is extremely important because it exerts a positive neurological influence on your brain. This helps counteract the negative self-esteem and shame that you may be experiencing.

Strategy 4: Celebrate Yourself on a Regular Basis

At first you may find it helpful to stop what you are doing at least once an hour (or even more frequently, if necessary) to celebrate yourself. Thinking negatively about yourself may be so ingrained as a habit that regular self-celebratory breaks are necessary to counteract them.

Strategy 5: Encourage Others to Celebrate Their Successes

There is a saying, "Teach what you want to learn."

Encouraging others to celebrate their successes rubs off on us.

Strategy 6: Be a Hero for Others

Many of us incorrectly believe that in order to be a hero, a person must accomplish some great feat. Going through the Talmud, writing a work of novel Torah insights, or running a large volunteer organization are many peoples' idea of truly heroic behavior. These indeed are wonderful accomplishments, but the Torah ideal of a hero is quite different. We are told in *Pirkei Avos* (4:1) that a hero who is one who conquers his or her *yetzer hara*. The depressed person has many opportunities to be that kind of hero. By choosing to get out of bed despite the weighty dread that holds you back, you are acting like a hero. By going for a walk when you feel tired, you are acting like a hero. And when others see you overcoming the symptoms of depression and they do the same, then you are helping them become heroes.

From the Author's Case Files

While checking my voice mail one day, I found a message from a friend of mine's rabbi. I had recently given a lecture in his shul. The rabbi requested that I call him, which I did right away.

After a bit of phone tag we finally made contact. The rabbi had a congregant who was both a friend and a supporter of the shul. Unfortunately, this man's daughter had recently gotten divorced and this hurt her father immensely. The man was depressed and despondent. Since the rabbi had liked what I had said at the lecture and my office was located out of the community, he asked if I would be willing to meet with his congregant. "Of course," I said. The rabbi said he would have the gentleman call me within the hour.

We set up an appointment for two days later. I really didn't think much of it. After all, I am not a stranger to depression. And I had other things to do in the meantime. The reason, however, that this story is memorable to me is because of what I encountered when I came back from my lunch break the day of the appointment. There was the rabbi in full regalia sitting next to the man, who I quickly learned was quite depressed.

I ushered the two of them into my office and tried to make heads or tails of what was going on. The man explained that his rabbi had become concerned with his welfare and therefore made him set up the appointment, drove him to it, and was now standing by to help. I got the picture pretty quickly. I also knew that with this rabbi in this man's life, this man was going to get better.

I excused the rabbi from the room for about an hour. I collected a history and the present level of symptoms. The man was indeed severely depressed but was not suicidal. The rabbi rejoined us and I told both of them that some psychotherapy would alleviate the depression. I also wanted the patient to be seen by a psychiatrist whom both men knew of. The rabbi again made his friend and congregant set up another appointment five days later.

Later that week, I got a call from the psychiatrist who asked me about the rabbi. I told him what had happened in my office. We both remarked on how fortunate this patient was to have this rabbi. Indeed, the psychiatrist did prescribe a well-known antidepressant and encouraged the patient to follow up with psychotherapy.

The patient and I began meeting twice a week. The rabbi actually drove him to the first few sessions. The first order of business was to work on improving his mood. This came through his use of the mood regulation strategies. He began walking (the rabbi and the man's wife had to drag him out of bed at first). He completed an activity scheduling form and with it got himself moving again.

Once he was less depressed, we could start addressing the psychological causes of his depression: namely, his daughter's divorce. We examined all of his beliefs about this sad event. He came to see clearly that it evoked all sorts of feelings of failure and shame on his part. Most important, on his own he was able to change many of his beliefs so that he could regain his sense of accomplishment and success.

Our therapy really didn't last that long. Given how severely he was depressed when I first met him, I would have thought that it would have lasted longer. But then again with a rabbi like that on your side, you just never know.

Chapter 5

Tackling Sleep Problems

Almost all depressed people complain of sleep difficulties. Most complain of being unable to get enough sleep. Some have difficulty falling asleep. Others find that they wake up long before they need to. There are also those depressed people who sleep excessively.

No universal biological explanation for the sleep problems of depression can be stated with certainty. Disruption of neurotransmitters such as serotonin and norepinephrine may very well be part of the cause of sleep disturbance. What is known, however, is that once you begin getting a better night's sleep and feel refreshed, you will probably have turned the corner on your depression. The good news is that many interventions are available to help get a good night's sleep. Sleeping medications are just the beginning. The sleep strategies in this chapter, when applied gently and consistently, will help you greatly.

Strategy 1: Seek Aggressive Treatment for Sleep Disturbance
Depressed patients seeking treatment for depres-

sion often focus primarily on their feelings and thoughts. These are understandably important problems to start with. Nevertheless, the relief of sleep disturbances is the first area that a well-educated patient should demand. Sleep deprivation or hypersomnia have great impact on your ability to fully benefit from treatment.

Evaluation for sleep disturbance depends on what you tell your clinician. Assessment usually involves some simple questions asked by a mental health professional. You may be given a form to fill out before and after you go to sleep. In some severe situations, you may be referred to a sleep center where your sleep patterns can be better examined.

In all cases, you will be asked about foods, medications, and activities that may affect your sleep. You may be counseled about sleep hygiene with some tailor-made recommendations offered. You may also be prescribed sleep medications. Follow your clinician's instructions and share questions and concerns that come up as your sleep improves.

Strategy 2: Check Your Diet

Evaluate your diet for foods that may be interfering with your sleep. Foods and beverages containing caffeine should be avoided at least four hours before you plan to go sleep. This includes foods that many people assume are caffeine free, such as chocolate and tea. In addition, avoid foods that contain other forms of stimulants such as ginseng or ephedra. Common examples are sports beverages and health bars.

Medications and over-the-counter remedies frequently interfere with sleep. Even antidepressant medications can cause insomnia. Consult with your clinician about the best times to take your medication. If you have sleep difficulties in spite of the reassurances of your clinician, respectfully request his or her input in finding some solution to this problem.

Strategy 3: Develop Sleep-supporting Rituals

Sleep rituals help your body make the transition from wakefulness to rest. These rituals should begin one hour before you intend to go to sleep. Light calisthenics or stretching, light reading, recitation of *Tehillim*, meditation, music, writing in a journal, or eating a light snack are examples of rituals. Reciting *Krias Shema* is an important ritual to help with relaxation and sleep.

At the same time, avoid eating, reading, or studying in your bed. Activities that wake you up will interfere with your sleep. Get into bed when you are ready to sleep and leave it when you rise. Otherwise, you may send your body conflicting cues for bedtime and waking life.

Strategy 4: Make Your Sleep Area Conducive to Sleep

By making the place that you sleep conducive to sleep you increase your odds of getting the rest that you need. Most of us require a room that is relatively free of noise. Politely ask people in your environment for their assistance. Inexpensive ear plugs can help prevent a great deal of noise from interfering with your sleep. You can also experiment with noise-canceling devices and sound machines. These devices generate sleep friendly sounds that mitigate the effect of sleep-robbing noise such as barking dogs, music, and so forth.

Temperature and humidity should be adjusted for your optimal comfort. Purchase or borrow any devices such as humidifiers or air conditioners that will help you feel comfortable. Eliminate dust or odors that irritate you. Make sure that your mattress is conducive to sleeping. In order to sleep, your body must be taken into account. If you cannot get physically comfortable, it will be next to impossible to settle yourself down mentally so that you get your needed rest. The expenses involved in improving your bedroom are well worth it.

Strategy 5: Know When to Get Out of Bed

If you find that you are having difficulty falling asleep, get out of bed. Tossing and turning for more than twenty minutes will only get you more frustrated. Instead, engage in a relaxing activity. You may find reading, reciting *Tehillim*, writing a journal, artwork, or studying to be just the thing to help you relax enough to get to sleep. Avoid worrying about the effects of sleep deprivation. Eventually, you will get the sleep that you need. You will be able to make it through the next day.

Strategy 6: Consider Using Sleep Medications

At some point you and your clinician may consider the use of medication to help you sleep. This is usually a wise decision. Sleep medications are an effective way to help you get needed rest. A rested mind and body are crucial for depression recovery.

There are two broad categories of medications: those that require a physician's prescription and those that don't. Prescription sleep medications can be further broken down into two groups: those that were manufactured specifically for sleep problems and those medications whose side effects cause sleepiness.

Medications made specifically for sleep are relatively recent additions to the long list of prescription medications. These pills are designed to induce sleep and not cause drowsiness during the day. Drug manufacturers claim that these medications are not addictive. Nevertheless, many people become psychologically dependent on them. Psychological dependence means that you believe that you will be unable to fall asleep without taking the pill.

If you are currently moderately to severely depressed and have experienced consistent insomnia, the fear of psychological dependence is *not* a reason to not take sleep medication. A competent and caring professional can always help you end your dependence on these medications. The benefits of a rested mind are more important than the risks posed by psychological dependence.

Prescription medications that cause sleepiness as a side effect are primarily psychiatric medications. Usually these are older antidepressants or antianxiety medications. The older antidepressants can cause some temporary unwanted side effects such as drowsiness during the day. Nevertheless, they can be especially helpful for patients who have not had success with other medications.

Nonprescription sleep medications include antihistamines and herbal remedies. Antihistamines, which are primarily used for allergies and colds, cause sleepiness as a side effect. They are included in almost all over-the-counter sleep remedies as well as in those pain remedies that claim to help you fall asleep as well. Many people have benefited from these sleep remedies. They have few side effects. It is vital to report your use of them to your clinician so that he or she can have a fuller picture of your health.

Herbal remedies for insomnia include melatonin, kava kava, and others. These supplements should be used with caution. The manufacturers of herbal and homeopathic remedies have little supervision. Their claims of safety and effectiveness have never been substantiated to the degree that prescription medications are. Side effects such as anxiety during the day or allergic reactions are not uncommon. For these reasons, most clinicians discourage the use of these remedies.

Some words of caution regarding sleep medications: Sleep medications of all types have been enormously helpful to countless depressed individuals. Nevertheless, some words of caution are necessary before you and your clinician consider going the medication route. First and foremost is that sleep medication may impede your depression recovery. This is the case when you are avoiding addressing the personal and psychological issues underlying your insomnia.

In addition, sleep medication should only be used after a complete physical evaluation for causes of insomnia. Medical disorders, lifestyle issues, and side effects of medications should all be ruled out as insomnia culprits. Prescribing sleep medication without adequate evaluation is poor medical practice.

Finally, sleep medications are intended for short-term use. The fact that many people appear to take these medications on a long-term basis is at odds with what the drug manufacturers state about their own products.

Tackling Sleep Problems

You owe it to yourself and your long-term health to find alternate ways to get the sleep you need.

Eleven Golden Tricks to Get to Sleep

The following are the most frequently suggested ways to get to sleep. Use them when you are going to sleep at the beginning of the night or if you wake up in the middle of the night.

Strategy 1: Get Some Exercise

One simple solution for insomnia is physical activity. Exercise releases pent-up stress. Even the most modest exercise several hours before sleep releases natural stimulants in your body. These stimulants will decrease your need for caffeine and will leave you more tired at bedtime.

Strategy 2: Have a Small Snack

Going to bed on an empty stomach usually interferes in getting to sleep. A small, light snack may help. However, avoid foods that may interfere with your digestion or give you heartburn.

Strategy 3: Try a Warm Beverage

Warm milk or decaffeinated herbal tea has been used by millions to induce sleep.

Strategy 4: Stick to a Regular Bedtime

Go to bed at about the same time every night. Set the alarm clock to awaken you at about the same time every morning, including weekends, regardless of the amount of sleep you have had. If you have a poor night's sleep, don't linger in bed or oversleep the next day. If you awaken before it is time to rise, get out of bed and start your day.

Strategy 5: Count Sheep

Counting sheep or some other neutral image is a time-honored way to lull yourself to sleep. Don't resist the thoughts that come into your head, but try not to follow them either. Instead, accept them and provide yourself with an alternative focus. Notice as the thoughts float into your consciousness; then observe as they float away.

Strategy 6: Count Breaths

Count inhalations and exhalations. When you reach five or ten, go back to one. Relax your breathing. Breathe as slowly and deeply as you comfortably can. There doesn't need to be any strain — only calmness and gratitude that you can rest now after all of the activity of the day.

Strategy 7: Use the Body Sweep

In this exercise you move your attention slowly up your body. As you pass over it with your awareness, flex and relax each muscle group that you pass. Avoid fighting off intrusive thoughts. Instead keep yourself detached from those thoughts, letting them depart rather than chewing them over.

Breathe slow and easy. Start at your toes. Flex your toes, and relax. Then flex your toes and your feet and relax. Then your toes, feet, and ankles, calves, and so forth. Feel your body getting heavier and sinking deeper into the mattress. Work up your belly and chest, and then move up your back. Then move your awareness from the fingertips to your hands, and up to the shoulders. From your shoulders, go up to the neck — contract all the muscles front and back, and feel the tension flow out as you release. Lastly, work up to your head and face.

Strategy 8: Be Careful with Naps

Naps can be a great pleasure. If they affect your regular sleep patterns, however, consider cutting back. Especially try to avoid nodding off at any time closer than seven or eight hours before your bedtime.

Strategy 9: Keep Your Clock to the Wall

When you go to bed, turn your alarm clock toward the wall so you don't worry about the time.

Strategy 10: Do Some Light Reading in Bed

A few minutes of light reading can help get your body in the mood for sleeping. Avoid thrillers or technical material that may activate you and interfere with sleep.

Strategy 11: Get Out of Bed

Avoid spending more than fifteen or twenty minutes trying to drift off to sleep. If you cannot sleep, get up and engage in some relaxing activity. If there is something on your mind, then try to do something about it. When you feel sufficiently drowsy, then go back to bed.

Strategies for Staying Asleep

Even when you can fall asleep, you may be unable to sleep long enough. You may find yourself waking up hours before you have to. Your efforts to fall asleep again are of no avail. Understandably, this pattern can become frustrating and frightening as you feel worse and worse due to sleep deprivation.

Fortunately you can intervene effectively in this pattern. The first step ideally should involve discussion with your mental health professional. He or she may recommend medication or further investigation of your particular sleep problem. In addition, the two of you may decide to experiment with some strategies to help you sleep through the night.

Consider some of the following strategies to help you sleep through the night.

Strategy 1: Make Your Sleep Environment Conducive to Sleeping through the Night

Identify sources of sound or light that interfere with your sleep. Does the temperature or humidity in your room make sleeping difficult? Without eliminating the tangible factors that get in the way of decent sleep, your other efforts will be undermined.

Strategy 2: Get Out of Bed

When you wake up and realize that you cannot get back to sleep, continuing to lie in your bed will frustrate you and make falling asleep again even more difficult. Get up and go sit down elsewhere. Even if you are not actually sleeping, relaxation alone will have a restorative effect.

Strategy 3: Engage in Relaxing Activity

By focusing your attention on a rhythmic, relaxing activity, you can gently prepare your body to return to sleep. Examples of such activities are reading, saying *Tehillim*, knitting, drawing, listening to gentle music, drinking some herbal tea, or meditating.

Strategy 4: Remember Your Dreams

Keep track of any significant dream activity you experience just prior to early awakening. Some people who awaken early while depressed have vivid dreams that are helpful in therapy. Share your experiences with your therapist.

Getting Up in the Morning When You Don't Feel Like It

Groan. Depressed people hate the morning. They greet the morning as yet another dreaded event. The new day represents further agony and opportunities to sink deeper into despair.

Nevertheless, it is only in the potential contained within the activities of the day that the building blocks of recovery lie. There is energy out there and the depressed person needs it to get better. Getting out of bed is the first step in accessing that healing power.

Ironically, getting out of bed in the morning begins the night before. Some easy planning is necessary. First things first: When do you want to get up? Set an alarm clock, ask friends to call you, do whatever you need to do in order to wake up.

The next step is to decide how you want to get up and out of bed in the morning. Do you want to awaken slowly and gradually? Would you like to get out of bed with great energy? Write a first-person, present-tense description of how you want to start your day on a piece of paper or in your recovery journal.

As an example you might write the following: "I wake up at the desired time with energy and optimism." Rewrite this declaration as many times as it takes to cut through any inner resistance that you encounter.

All depressed adults have at least a few emotional reasons why this declaration is unrealistic or ridiculous.

REASONS TO STAY IN BED	COUNTERSTATEMENTS
It's so comfortable in bed.	Yes, it is comfortable; however, if I continue to avoid my life it will not only be uncomfortable but frightening as well. I will surrender to the fact that as I get moving I will find some minor comfort in the activities of my day.
I will have no energy.	As I slowly merge into the flow of life, my energy will gently increase without my awareness. Count on a "second wind" of energy as you move.
I am scared of....	Yes, there are many frightening things out there. But I need not tackle them all today. In fact, remaining in my bed is no more safe than being up and about.
What if I fail?	Failing is different from being a failure. As I am a work in progress, I am never a failure. God doesn't make failures. Failure is part of the process of succeeding. All failures that I encounter will remind me that I am on the way to succeeding.
I just want to sleep for another ten minutes, thirty minutes, hour, etc.	Sleep as long as you want. But remember that while your depression head has lured you into thinking that sleep is what you need, your *neshamah* knows that accomplishment is what you want.

Each repetition of the declaration brings up new reasons. Write these reasons down. In order to move forward with your plan to get up, you will need to dispute these counterstatements sufficiently so that they do not interfere in the morning. Share these counterstatements with your psychotherapist. You can also dispute these counterstatements on your own. Consider the examples of disputations in the table on the previous page.

Once you have programmed your mind and addressed all of the dysfunctional thoughts, you are ready to take the final steps before going to sleep. Arrange all of the clothing that you intend to wear tomorrow. If you intend to bathe, have everything that you will need ready to go. For those who enjoy drinking coffee in the morning, set your coffee maker timer so that you will awaken to the sweet smell of fresh-brewed coffee. If certain music invigorates you, then have a CD player or tape deck next to your bed so that you can easily turn it on as soon as you open your eyes. Set up everything that you will need in the morning. Say *Krias Shema Al HaMitah* with gentle focus on those verses that address the restoration of life and energy. See you in the morning!

From the Author's Case Files

> *When I first saw Yoni in my waiting room, my first thought was He's exhausted! I ushered him into my office and began an initial workup. Sometimes, looks are not deceiving. He indeed was utterly tired and beaten. He had come for psychotherapy because he had been depressed ever since he had started a new job. He had also not slept through the night in two months.*
>
> *Yoni was amenable to seeing a psychiatrist that I recommended. It was my impression that Yoni's sleeplessness and other physical symptoms would be especially helped by a psychiatric consultation. The psychiatrist did prescribe a well-known antidepressant*

and some sleep medication. All three of us agreed, however, that the sleep medication should only be used for one month or until Yoni could sleep adequately without them.

In the next month, Yoni and I focused on getting his sleep in order. He started a low-impact exercise program of walking each day. He regularly practiced some of the centering techniques that I taught him. In two weeks he reported that he was able to sleep through the night with only half of the sleeping pill. Of course, we worked on the issues that started his spiral into depression. His performance anxiety, fear of being laid off again, and other worries evoked great feelings of helplessness and hopelessness. But once he started getting some rest, half the battle was won.

Chapter 6

Tackling Appetite Disturbances

Given the connection between the mind and body, it should be no surprise that the appetite of a depressed person will be out of balance. Usually the depressed person has a poor appetite and loses weight. Since life has lost its flavor, food loses its appeal. Even favorite foods mean nothing to the depressed person.

However, increased appetite and weight gain is not uncommon. Appetite increase is more common when the depressed person also has physical agitation. It may also be a way of coping with anxiety. As you find it easier to relax your body, you will find it easier to cut back on the amount of food that you consume.

Because of the very different needs of those with poor appetites and those with increased appetites, strategies for both are presented separately.

For Those with Decreased Appetite

A healthy body is a prerequisite for recovery from depression. Nutrition is therefore an important part of improving your physical health and mental health. Your mental health care provider will be an excellent source of information about beneficial changes in your diet. For those who have reduced appetite these strategies will help.

Strategy 1: Dispute Your Reasons for Not Eating

Depressed people may eat less because of feelings of worthlessness or guilt. If you believe that depriving your body of food is a way to atone for misdeeds or a way to come closer to Hashem, you are mistaken. Poor nutrition undermines your health and energy, both of which are necessary for your service of Hashem. It is impossible to do *teshuvah* if you are malnourished.

Strategy 2: Reduce Your Anxiety

Consider the influence of anxiety on your appetite. It is understandably difficult to have any interest in food when you are panicked and anxious. Anxious people often feel nauseous. Many of the strategies in this book will help you reduce your anxiety. Discuss your anxiety and nausea with your health care professional.

Strategy 3: Check Your Medications

Are your medications part of the problem? Discuss this possibility with your mental health care professional. Consider experimenting with taking your medications at different times or after having something to eat.

Strategy 4: Take a Walk

Take a gentle walk before you eat. A five- or ten-minute stroll in fresh air will stimulate your appetite.

Tackling Appetite Disturbances

Strategy 5: Don't Limit Your Eating Further

Now is not the time to diet! First things first. Get healthy first and then you can safely focus on losing weight. Guilt feelings that you have regarding food or regarding your weight must be discussed with your psychotherapist. Go easy on yourself. Integrate your negative attitude toward your body with your depression recovery.

Strategy 6: Try Grazing

Eat small amounts of food six to eight times a day. Small, frequent meals or snacks prevent an early sense of fullness, and more food can be eaten over a twenty-four-hour period.

Strategy 7: Drink More Water

While it is not clear what the connection is, depressed and anxious people tend to drink less water. Keep yourself well hydrated with fresh, clean water. You may find that the clean feeling that you get after drinking water is an appetite stimulant.

Strategy 8: Eat Calmly

Eat your meals in a relaxed, pleasant setting. Such an environment is conducive to healthy eating.

Strategy 9: Eat Healthy Foods

Choose nutritious carbohydrates and high-protein options such as fish, chicken, turkey, eggs, cheeses, milk, ice cream, tofu, nuts, peanut butter, yogurt, beans, or peas. Experiment with many of the nutritious canned milk shakes and power drinks that are now available.

Strategies for Those with Increased Appetite

Strategy 1: Don't Use Pressure

Go easy on yourself! While it is understandable that you want to look and feel your best, now is not the time to worry about food and how much you eat.

Strategy 2: Gradually Include Healthier Foods

Don't stop yourself from eating at first. Gradually include healthier food in your daily diet. That way when you begin the process of changing your dietary habits you already have healthful foods in there.

Strategy 3: Drink More Water

While it is not clear what the connection is, depressed and anxious people tend to drink less water. Keep yourself well hydrated with fresh, clean water.

Strategy 4: Keep an Unfood Log

Write down all of the foods that you did not eat today. Celebrate yourself! This is one way to boost your self-confidence.

From the Author's Case Files

Shmuel was a single, twenty-four-year-old graduate student. He regularly attended a shiur given by an acquaintance of mine. My acquaintance's wife noticed that Shmuel seemed withdrawn during his frequent Shabbos visits. She and her husband decided to find out what was going on. It emerged that Shmuel was depressed. He readily accepted their recommendation to come see me.

Tackling Appetite Disturbances

When Shmuel and I met, I saw a gifted young man with fine middos. I also saw a young man who was clinically depressed. As I did my workup, I asked him about his physical health. He had some minor aches and pains which in someone of his youth were reflective of his depression. I queried him about his energy level. He said that it was poor. This led me to ask him about his diet. He told me flat out that he wasn't eating. Because it was winter, he was dressed in bulky clothes, so I was unable to tell if he was abnormally thin. But with the two-hundred-calorie diet he told me about, he must have been emaciated.

His restrictive diet was related to the simple fact that he had no desire to eat. He also admitted that there was an element of self-punishment involved in restricting his food intake. Aware that there would be little improvement in his depression without addressing his diet first, I invested the balance of the session on exploring how Shmuel could start eating again.

We discussed his beliefs about the necessity for self-punishment. I assumed that there was little utility in introducing strategies for improving his appetite without first debunking his reasons for not eating. The truth is that Shmuel needed little convincing that regardless of how unworthy he perceived himself, he could not avoid the fact that halachah clearly supported the importance of self-care. Ultimately we did need to explore his guilt for perceived misdeeds in greater detail. However, once Shmuel was able to sever the connection between guilt and eating he resumed a regular pattern of eating. A major part of the battle was won.

*   *   *

Moshe was a forty-seven-year-old rebbe in a yeshivah day school. He was referred to me by his health insurance company. Moshe told me that he believed he was having a reoccurrence of depression. He had had an episode of depression several years before, after his mother passed away. He had been in treatment with a colleague of mine, who had since moved out of the area. The therapy, he told me, had been helpful, and he wanted to use it again.

We started with a basic workup. Moshe was in fact moderately depressed. But what really struck me was the anxiety that he described. He was preoccupied with worries about his job security. He was worried about his son who appeared to be having a hard time at his yeshivah. The list went on and on. And he not only worried in his mind. He reported many of the physical symptoms of anxiety as well.

The only thing that seemed to help him calm down was eating. He described episodes of binging on cookies, cakes, and all sorts of plentiful carbohydrates. This binging embarrassed him greatly.

We initially focused on boosting his mood. I believed that once we helped him feel more energized, the anxiety symptoms could be dealt with more expeditiously. We worked on self-monitoring techniques. Moshe quickly learned the cognitive therapy technique of self-talk. He completed homework assignments in which I asked him to identify his destructive thoughts and replace them with more positive ones.

After six sessions, Moshe reported that he was be-

ginning to consistently feel better. He reported that he was using the self-talk technique for his worries as well. He wanted to know, in fact, if our therapy could focus more on his anxiety. Of particular concern was his eating because his doctor had told him that his blood pressure was a bit high.

Moshe followed my recommendations and began to exercise regularly by walking in the evening with his wife. He began to drink more water. I recommended that he read any mainstream nutrition book that he could find at the local library. I also recommended that for a few days he keep an "unfood log," a list of things that he didn't eat during the day. Within two weeks Moshe told me that things were coming together for him. He was feeling more energized, much less anxious, and proud of the fact that he was more in control of his eating.

Chapter 7

Tackling Hopelessness and Pessimism

> But you have not called upon Me, Yaakov; but you have been weary of Me, Yisrael.
> (*Yeshayah* 43:22)

What does the prophet mean that we became weary of Hashem, when in fact we never called upon Him?

The Maggid of Dubno answered with this parable: A guest at a hotel asked a bellhop to take his luggage to his room. When the bellhop returned, the guest went over to offer him a tip. He asked the worker if he had brought the bags to his room. The bellhop answered that he had, in fact, delivered two very heavy suitcases. The guest became quite alarmed. "If the suitcases were heavy, then they were not mine. My suitcases were quite light. You must have taken the wrong suitcases!"

Many people regrettably claim to find serving Hashem heavy and burdensome. They find it associated with guilt and harsh self-denial. For them service of God is quite weary. But the holy prophet, Yeshayah, tells us that this is not true service of God. If we are finding serving God difficult, then we have lost our way. True service of God is with joy and hope.

Depression affects thinking abilities. When in the grip of depression our ability to make heads or tails of reality deteriorates. We become intellectually slower. Our memories fail us, except with regards to events that lower us deeper and deeper into depression. These destructive patterns of thinking lead to hopelessness and pessimism. Hopelessness and pessimism lead to passivity because, after all, what is the use of trying? And this deadly beat goes on as you sink deeper and deeper into the pit of despair.

The good news is that the pessimism and hopelessness of depression have been extensively studied. We know more about these destructive thought patterns than we ever have. Scientific understanding has led to methods of resetting thinking styles even among people who have been depressed for many years. These thinking habits can be broken. They can be replaced with a way of thinking that gives you strength, optimism, and freedom. The following strategies will get you started on claiming the personal power and optimism that is rightly yours.

Spices and Habits of Depression

Reality is neutral. What one person thinks is a positive event someone else will see as a negative one. A cracked window is an aggravation to one person and an opportunity to make some money for another. A failed *shidduch* is a great disappointment for one person and a new opportunity for another. Death is the ultimate catastrophe for one person, but the opportunity to reap the rewards of a life well lived for another. In the end, it is our beliefs about an event that lead us to view it as negative or positive.

How we think about any event is kind of like adding spices to food. When you spice food, you take a neutral food and you add a spice to it. The spice adds a flavor that wasn't present in the food before. Or the addition of a spice may strengthen a flavor that was already there. A spice may neutralize the other tastes. Some foods may have a naturally strong taste and require a lot of spices to overcome that natural flavor.

In the last thirty years researchers have looked more and more at the spices that depressed people add to objective reality. These spices are called cognitive styles. What intrigued researchers was the fact that you could expose groups of similar people to the same events and end up with so many different reactions. The researchers concluded that depressed people do things to events that nondepressed people don't do. And depressed people don't do things that nondepressed people do.

So what are these spices that depressed people add to events? What makes them more vulnerable to sadness, hopelessness, and passivity? What are the strategies that nondepressed people use that depressed people don't? How can depressed people stop adding the spices and start using the strategies of nondepressed people? Stay tuned because here it comes!

The Spices of Depression Thinking

Researchers who spent thousands of hours listening to how depressed people talked about negative events in their lives found that depressed people tend to use one or more of the following spices almost all of the time.

These spices are:

- Catastrophizing
- Minimizing
- Perfectionistic thinking
- Self-referenced thinking
- Labeling
- Jumping to conclusions
- Blaming

Catastrophizing refers to the assumption that any form of adversity or negative event is catastrophic. In colloquial language, it refers to making a mountain out of a molehill. Depressed people engage in this type of thinking often enough that they become overwhelmed. And why shouldn't they? In their mind, a catastrophe has occurred.

Minimization is the flip side of catastrophizing. Depressed people tend to dismiss positive events and actions as inconsequential. Depressed people are unable to value the small steps that are necessary for achievement. And because the small steps or tiny little positives in life are the building blocks of hope and recovery, the depressed person fails to use them.

Perfectionistic thinking is a constant expectation that anything of value must be perfect. Efforts must be perfect. Appearances must be perfect. And so on. I always tell my patients that there are certainly times for perfection. We would all agree that a car mechanic should perfectly repair worn brakes. The depressed person, however, demands perfection of self and others in many kinds of activities. Not getting the desired level of perfection leaves the depressed person frequently disappointed and angry. Or he or she may refrain from taking some sort of action because of the erroneous belief that the effort must be perfect. This results in even greater passivity.

Self-referenced thinking refers to the tendency to relate to an event based on one's current mood and past experiences. Depressed people tend to see even positive events as negative in some way. Since they are looking at life through lenses clouded with negativity and pessimism, they easily find reasons for more negativity and pessimism in almost everything that they look at.

Labeling refers to the depressed person's tendency to categorize a person, experience, or object based on a very limited track record. Labels are almost always negative. Slipping on a walkway ends up becoming a label of "I'm such a klutz." Not understanding a *shiur* means that "I am just stupid." If I cannot fit into some clothing, then "I am a fat slob." Labels are certainly applied to others as well. What makes labels so harmful is that they are simplistic conclusions that eliminate the possibility of any improvement.

Jumping to conclusions is the tendency to conclude that an event is negative before all of the facts are in. Depressed people seem to have a lot of difficulty waiting until all of the data is amassed. They therefore jump to a conclusion, usually a negative one. "He didn't call the *shadchan* yet; he must not be interested in going out again." "The interviewer hasn't called me, so they don't want me." "My neighbor in shul didn't respond to my greeting. I must have offended him."

Blaming is the tendency to misapply responsibility. Depressed people almost always blame themselves or others when an adverse event happens. Perversely, even when they accomplish something positive, they "blame" others or luck for it. Most of the time they are confused about the degree of control that they or anyone else has over life. Because of this confusion and exaggerated belief of control, they are often angry and frustrated. This anger and frustration can also lead to a protective stance of indifference and passivity.

The Cognitive Spices of the Nondepressed Person

Wait and see the salvation of Hashem.
(*Divrei HaYamim* II 20:17)

Depressed people and nondepressed people encounter the same adversities in life. Whereas the depressed person is adding his dark spices, however, the nondepressed person adds his or her own spices to the event. For the nondepressed, adversity becomes manageable. In fact, the event can become one of the many positive points in the life of the nondepressed person.

The nondepressed person's cognitive spices are:

- Curiosity

- Surrender to a Higher Will

- Magnification of opportunities

- Awareness of strengths

- Sense of humor

Curiosity refers to the nondepressed person's insatiable curiosity about adversity. He or she looks for the unexpected in the event. Whereas the depressed person jumps to conclusions about adversity, the nondepressed person is waiting to see how things develop. A nondepressed person will often say to himself, *I wonder how this is going to turn out* or *This is where it gets interesting.* He wonders what spiritual, emotional, physical, or social benefits will come from this adversity. Because he remains curious, he is open to the gifts and opportunities available and those that may appear.

Surrender to a Higher Will refers to the nondepressed person's ability to change his agenda, needs, and desires to that of God. He or she recognizes that Hashem's will is wiser. In fact, Hashem as our Heavenly Father knows what is best for us better than we could ever hope to understand. Even when the adversity seems incomprehensible, the nondepressed person accepts his inability to comprehend. He is willing to give Hashem the benefit of the doubt. While the nondepressed person may respond emotionally to an adverse event, she or he can quickly regain peace of mind and focus. Adversity for the nondepressed person is like a blow to the stomach — it hurts, but when the hurt goes away, he straightens up and resumes living.

Magnification of opportunities refers to the nondepressed person's habit of focusing on the opportunities in the adversity. Instead of magnifying the hardships and hassles, the nondepressed person is busy taking advantage of the adversity for his or her own spiritual, emotional, physical, or financial benefit. Nondepressed people can seize opportunities that others are not aware of. They can also validate the efforts that they make to address the adversity even when those efforts are not fully effective.

Awareness of strengths is the nondepressed person's ability to summon up skills and strengths that he knows he has. Whether it is the ability to break down problems and tasks into manageable units or the ability to reach out to others for help, the nondepressed person knows what he can do and does it. He is also aware of what may be missing from his repertoire. He is willing to ask others for help or to develop those skills for himself.

Sense of humor is the nondepressed person's habit of finding humor even in the toughest of adversities. Humor cannot make any tragedy easier. It helps make the situation easier to bear by giving an alternate way of looking at it. When you can laugh at an event, you can have power over it.

The Cognitive Habits of the Depressed Person

Depressed people have habits of thinking that sabotage their ability to cope with any form of adversity. These habits all reduce the depressed person's ability to respond to the needs of the moment. This results in increased feelings of powerlessness and incapacity.

These habits are

- Bearing trouble alone
- Preoccupation with feelings
- Reacting instead of creating
- Resistance to change

Bearing trouble alone is the most destructive of the negative habits of the depressed person. When we encounter adversity in the company of someone else we have the combined resources of two or more people. The depressed person does not have someone whom he can turn to. His ability to deal with adversity by himself is much more limited. He sees fewer solutions. He feels much more overwhelmed. The adversity becomes one more proof of his ineffectiveness. This leads to deeper levels of depression.

Preoccupation with feelings is the compulsion of the depressed person to overvalue his or her feelings. Feelings for the depressed person define what he can do or cannot do. Feelings define his or her reality. A feeling that "someone doesn't like me" goes unchallenged because it is a feeling. The feeling that others will reject me "because I am too fat" is accepted as fact. The disaster of a preoccupation with feelings is obvious. Feelings are expressions of what is already inside of us, not of the potential that lies outside. Growth and success lie in the balancing act between thinking and feeling.

Reacting instead of creating refers to the depressed person's tendency to remain passive to his or her detriment. The nondepressed person is proactive and creative in addressing needs and adversities. The depressed person, on the other hand, waits and waits until a small problem becomes a gigantic crisis. By putting actions off, the depressed person is in a much poorer position to solve a pressing need.

Resistance to change refers to the depressed person's unwillingness to change in order to meet the needs of the present. "You cannot teach an old dog new tricks" is the motto of the depressed person. He or she is therefore surprised and overwhelmed when old, outdated ways of handling adversity are unable to fix things now.

The Cognitive Habits of the Nondepressed Person

Even nondepressed people have pessimistic moments. They, too, may add some of the depressed spices to adverse events. What prevents the nondepressed person from slipping into negativity are cognitive habits that cancel out the spices. These habits are most often learned in childhood. The good news is that you can develop these habits at any point in your life.

These life-giving cognitive habits are:

- Asking questions about how they are experiencing an event
- Talking to others about the event
- Dislike of negative feelings
- The ability to regulate their feelings

Asking questions means that you can step outside your feelings and reactions. You can question the accuracy of your response. You can ask yourself whether your initial responses to the problems were effective. You can ask yourself whether other strategies might be even more effective. You can ask yourself how others might address the same problem.

Talking about the event with others means reaching out to someone and sharing your worries and feelings. It means opening up just enough so that you can receive validation. It means requesting and receiving feedback.

RETURNING TO JOY

Unfortunately, depressed people don't have people in their lives to talk to. They experience excessive shame, shyness, or anxiety about how others will respond. Catastrophic thinking and other spices undermine their ability to reach out to others.

Dislike of negative feelings refers to the nondepressed person's desire to return to a positive feeling state as quickly as possible. The depressed person often savors a bad mood. He or she may find power in ruminating about the hurts caused by others. The nondepressed person cannot stand bad moods because they don't really accomplish anything. They prefer joy and power to hatred and jealousy. If wronged, they confront and forgive the guilty party. When beset by a financial difficulty, they work hard to resolve the problem as quickly and aggressively as they can. They often encounter initial failure. Because of their motivation to succeed, however, they eventually succeed. This leaves them plenty of time to do those things that they enjoy. They can have the feelings that they want to have.

The ability to regulate emotions means that feelings need not be totally in charge of life. Nondepressed people have feelings. When necessary, however, they have skills that they use to exert control over those feelings. They can put their feelings in their back pocket and use their rational side to address the needs at hand.

Nondepressed people also have the ability to generate positive feelings when they want to. They can joke with friends, exercise, dance, sing, or say *Tehillim* to lift their spirits. They can write out their feelings because they realize that the ability to express a feeling means that the feeling can be controlled. They can eat a healthy

Tackling Hopelessness and Pessimism

meal or care for their bodies because they realize that feelings can run away when the body is weakened. They have music at their fingertips that boosts their moods. They interact with at least one other positive, uplifting person each day.

How to Stop Spicing Your Depression

Awareness of the cognitive spices alone won't stop you from adding them to the events of your life. Catching yourself when you have added them is only the first step. Replacing those spices is the key to changing a negative event into a neutral or positive event.

1. Event, date, and time	
2. Feelings (use feeling list)	
3. Dominant depressed person's cognitive spices and habits	
4. Alternate nondepressed person's cognitive spices habits	
5. Desired feelings (use feeling list)	
6. Positive action plan	

The best technique for eliminating depressed thinking is the use of a thought-recording form. While you can develop your own if you wish, the above sample form is one that many patients have found helpful. I recommend to my patients that they complete three forms in between sessions. This helps them begin getting into the habit of thinking about how they can add different spices to the adversities of life.

In row 1 write down the facts of the event as you can recall them. As you go through the form you may recall more details. Add those in as they come up. What is often fascinating is how our recollection of a troubling event changes as our mood changes for the better.

Consider the words of Malka, twenty-nine, wife, mother of three, and part-time teacher:

While visiting with my parents my older sister did something that upset me. I used that event for my thought record. After writing down what happened, I was interrupted by the baby. When I returned to the sheet later in the day, I noticed that there were two important details that I had left out. More importantly, I wasn't so angry at my sister anymore.

In row 2 write down your feelings related to the event. You may be able to identify one feeling or several feelings. I recommend that you use the list of feelings in appendix A. Going through this list will assure that you are aware of all your feelings.

Consider the words of Shlomo, thirty-nine, husband, father of four, and engineer:

The event involved a distressing meeting that I had with

Tackling Hopelessness and Pessimism

my boss about my year-end review. At first I named "anger" as the only feeling that I had. When I looked at the list, however, I noticed that I had other feelings as well. I felt ashamed, embarrassed, fearful, and panicky.

In row 3, write down the cognitive spices involved in your negative feelings and beliefs. Review the list of spices. Examine each of your feelings and thoughts. Are any of your feelings and thoughts inaccurate or overly pessimistic?

Shlomo continues:

As soon as I thought about the event, I knew I was jumping to conclusions. My supervisor never said that I was going to be demoted. Yet I reacted as though that was going to happen. When I reviewed the event with my therapist, I also realized that I had minimized the positive things that the supervisor had said about my performance. I also catastrophized about the importance of the whole event because, after all, it was highly unlikely that I would get fired.

Row 4 requires that you think differently about the event. Review the nondepressed person's spices and habits. How might they be helpful? Ask yourself how someone else might respond. How would someone of whom you think highly react to the adversity? Think of a time when you felt more powerful or more in control. In your mind, go back to that time and then look at the event that you are experiencing through the prism of that event. How would you respond differently from that more powerful vantage point?

Malka continues:

During seminary I was a counselor in a post–high school girls' program in Jerusalem. I ran a small discussion group for some of the girls. We all became very close. I felt really good about myself at that time. In fact, since then I don't think I have ever felt as happy. I was a role model and they looked up to me on how to handle life. So I looked at the event with my sister through the good feeling that I once had. I imagined that I was going to tell those girls how I gave my sister the benefit of the doubt. And do you know what? I was able to!

In row 5 write down how you would rather feel in this moment. If you want, you can also write down how you wish you could feel about the event itself. Otherwise, simply write down feelings that you would prefer to have now. Use the feelings list in appendix A to help you select your desired feeling or feelings.

Malka continues:

I decided that I wanted to feel forgiving and less burdened.

In row 6 think of some activities that you can do now to get to those positive feelings. Who can you go to for advice? Have you addressed similar adversities before? Can you utilize your past experiences in this case? What must you change about yourself? What is your plan to execute that change?

Shlomo continues:

I decided that I was probably reacting so emotionally to the year-end review because I was tired and hungry. I decided that the best plan of action was to get some exercise, since that always energizes me, and then have

> dinner. I went for a brisk walk. While walking I felt as though the depression and fear were receding into the past. The lively music I was listening to helped me move even faster. When I came home we all had dinner and after maariv I went to sleep. End of story.

Malka continues:

> I decided that I wanted to use opposite action to improve my relationship with my sister. My sister loves a certain candy bar that had just come under rabbinical supervision. I went to the store, bought a small bag for twenty-five cents, and mailed it to her. She called me up three days later to thank me. We kidded around for a little while on the phone. It was the best conversation we had had in a long time.

Other Techniques for Developing Optimism and Hope

Strategy 1: Find a Healthy Environment

> "What is the evil way that a person should avoid?"... Rabbi Yosei answered, "A bad neighbor."
>
> (*Avos* 2:9)

The first step in developing a more optimistic outlook is to avoid environments that strengthen your pessimism. Naysayers, criticizers, and negative people will make your efforts so much harder. Refrain from inviting pessimism into your home. This means shutting off the television and other sources of negativity.

Find positive people to associate with. You can find them in shul, at a *shiur*, or in some volunteer group. You can find them at work or in class. They may not be perfect people. They may not be people you wish to be friendly with. Nevertheless, they are working toward a better future, even if that future is much different than the one you are striving for.

Obviously you cannot suddenly leave or change a negative environment, especially when you are married to or dependent on the members of that environment. In fact, you don't even need to leave them or change them. What you do need to do is to focus on maintaining your sanity. Your mental health is your business. Maintaining sanity means that you are aware of the insanity of pessimism and that your true essence is hopeful and optimistic. You can use the negativity and pessimism of others as an inspiration to strive for deeper levels of optimism.

Strategy 2: Check Your Heroes and Role Models

> Rabbi Yosei ben Kisma said: Once I was walking by the way when a man greeted me and said to me, "Rabbi, from where do you come?" I said to him, "From a great city of sages and scribes." He said to me, "Rabbi, if you wish to dwell in our place, I will give you a thousand denarii of gold and precious stones and pearls." I said to him: "If you gave me all the silver and gold, precious stones, and pearls in the world, I would not dwell anywhere except in a place of Torah."
>
> (*Avos* 6:9)

A pessimistic, perfectionistic, or depressed parent or a verbally abusive teacher can shape a destructive self-image that lasts a lifetime. The beliefs that we absorb from the "heroes" in our lives can either make us or break us. This is even the case when we have not followed in the lifestyle of these individuals.

Review the influential people in your life. Which attitudes have you taken to be your own? How you handle minor imperfections, rejections, irritations, anger, food, and countless other parts of life may go back to these role models. By examining how the important people in your life have influenced you in the present, you can make some important decisions. You can decide whether these values and attitudes work for you and allow you to experience joy or if they undermine you.

Find new heroes and role models. Outside our community many people have written their struggles and triumphs. It may be hard for a Torah-observant Jew to find heroes within our community who speak openly about their struggles with depression. But they are out there. Learn from their example and be a hero to others.

Strategy 3: Minding the Mind-Body Connection

Let's face it. It is impossible to think clearly if you are undernourished or poorly rested. Optimism is a lot easier to obtain when you are in good physical condition. So if you find yourself thinking pessimistic thoughts, ask yourself if your physical condition is to blame. If it is then eat a nutritious meal or get some sleep. Then come back to the adversity. You may find that the situation looks different when your body is ready.

Strategy 4: Think on Purpose

Thinking for depressed people is a painful activity. Depressed people think about whatever comes into their awareness. When they wake up and find that it's raining they think about the rain. "Oh no, it's raining! I have to stand in the rain in my suit! I am going to be cold!

I will get to work sopping." This train of thought leads to other depressing trains of thought. And so it goes. One negative thought leads to another all day long.

You can break this deadly beat. You can think on purpose. Decide what you want to think about. You may want to think of verses from Tanach or statements of our Sages. You may want to think about goals that you have. The more that you focus on what you want, the more your mind works toward bringing those things into existence.

As an example of this technique in action, I keep my list of goals in my pocket. I review these goals throughout the day. This gives me the opportunity to refocus my thoughts on where I want them to be. Consider writing down a list of uplifting thoughts on an index card. Place the card in your pocket. Review those thoughts as often as you can.

I often give my patients an assignment of writing down five to seven uplifting thoughts on an index card. They are then to set an inexpensive digital kitchen timer for eighteen minutes. Every eighteen minutes when the alarm goes off they are to read the inspirations aloud. Sometimes I ask them to write these phrases in their recovery notebook. They are to write down any counterthoughts that they might have about them. We then discuss these exercises at our next session.

Consider the inspiring words of Ben, forty-seven, husband and father of five, attorney:

> *One of the cue phrases that I chose was "Envy, desire, and the desire for honor remove a person from this world" (Avos 4:21). This was because I realized that my envy of others' financial wealth was undermining*

my mental health. *As I reviewed this statement of Rav Elazar HaKapar, I realized that I wasn't so sure why envy was such a terrible thing. I knew it was a destructive character trait, but it just seemed that without jealousy people would not push themselves. This led me to think some more about bitachon and how I can serve Hashem in a more positive manner. All of this came through the exercise recommended by my therapist.*

Strategy 5: Advertise to Yourself

"*Shema Yisrael*" is a verse that the Torah wants us to remember. We wear it in our tefillin. We put it on our doors. We say it a minimum of three times a day. By demanding that we review and repeat this central mitzvah so many times every day, the Torah is demonstrating a powerful tool for self-development. That tool is repetition.

Repetition is a way for you to change the way you think. It is a powerful method to focus on your highest self instead of your misery. Wisdoms, verses, music, even jokes that inspire you must be repeated over and over again. The more you repeat and advertise to yourself, the deeper and the more natural your optimism and power will become.

Summary

Hopelessness and pessimism are barriers to exiting from the grips of your depression. They have their roots in the way that you think. Most likely, you had some of the pessimistic ways of thinking well before you became depressed. The habit of pessimism led to passivity and helplessness, which led to depression. The good news is that this habit can be broken. An optimistic style of thinking will provide the basis for long-term recovery from depression.

From the Author's Case Files

Sarah was a single twenty-two-year-old who was referred to me by a local psychiatrist in a nearby community. Her parents had forced her to see the psychiatrist because of a change in her behavior. According to the records that were forwarded to me, Sarah was often irritable and insensitive to the feelings of other family members. The psychiatrist recommended medication, which Sarah agreed to take. The doctor also recommended some psychotherapy, which Sarah also reluctantly agreed to.

I was surprised that Sarah could ever have been described as irritable. In our first sessions she appeared to be eager to offer information and was full of smiles. Of course, I assumed that the social niceties would soon be replaced by a more authentic version of Sarah. I was not long in waiting. The session began with some questions about her personal goals in life. They were curiously vague and lacking. I assumed that work and marriage would be on the agenda, but they weren't. As gently as I could, I asked about those goals. I was met with a polite but vigorous dismissal. I probed a bit further and the response became more intense.

At that point in the session I took a step back and asked Sarah what exactly was going on. She was clearly distressed about my question, and I invited her to tell me what had set her off. What emerged was a deep sense of hopelessness and pessimism about her life.

Tackling Hopelessness and Pessimism

On one hand, she very much wanted to start a family and follow up on a long-standing interest in a finance degree. On the other, she had met with what she perceived to be failure and gave up. The cool, rugged, and angry pose that she assumed was a kind of cover that she used to protect herself from disappointment.

It took a lot of creativity and hard work to crack that armor of pessimism. We spoke often of her heroes and how they had coped with setbacks. We discovered setbacks in her own short life that she had mastered. Sarah came to realize how parts of American culture often poisons optimism. She was sent home with an assignment to interview her grandmother about how she coped with some of the obstacles that she encountered. After a few sessions Sarah was beginning to see her pessimism in its true light: a cop-out from trying.

The battle had only just begun, however. Sarah's tendency to spice neutral events as negative was a long-standing habit. She did, however, agree to the thought-monitoring forms that I recommended. She worked hard at catching herself when she retreated from life by minimizing her successes or catastrophizing obstacles. Over the course of a year of weekly psychotherapy, Sarah developed a healthy and flexible optimism. The last time I heard from her, she had resumed dating and was in graduate school.

Chapter 8

Tackling Increased or Decreased Energy

Your head is connected to your body. Depression not only affects the way that your mind works; it disrupts your physiology as well. A common manifestation of the physical side of depression is in your energy level. Your energy may be low. Performing the simplest tasks becomes difficult. You may also feel agitated and uncomfortable inside your own skin. The following strategies will help your find the optimum level of comfort and energy.

For Those with Decreased Energy

Strategy 1: Get a Physical

If you haven't had a physical recently, now is the time to do so. Your depleted physical energy may be related to some underlying physical cause. A thorough physical can help you make lifestyle changes in diet and exercise that support the level of energy you want.

Strategy 2: Get Physical

Objects in motion stay in motion. Objects at rest stay

Tackling Increased or Decreased Energy

at rest. The same rules apply to physical energy. If you desire more energy, then the only way to generate it is to move. All of the following psychological and spiritual techniques arrive at the inescapable fact: action comes from action. There is no way to avoid this.

Strategy 3: Disarm the Fears that Keep You Out of Action

After having been depressed for any period of time, it seems as though physical activity is absolutely beyond your capacity. All sorts of fears about physical activity have had time to develop. With time these fears have become magnified. While disarming these fears does not inherently result in an increase in energy, your intellectual awareness that these fears are bogus makes the process possible. The following page has a list of the most common fears that depressed adults have about physical activity. Next to each you will find counterstatements that patients have discovered on the way to increasing their physical activity.

Strategy 4: Set Yourself Up to Succeed

Increasing your energy doesn't just happen. It involves overcoming enough of the negative fears described above. Activity scheduling is the next step toward getting your energy back. Physically writing down what you plan to do in advance serves to imprint the activity into your psyche. In fact, I often recommend to my patients that they rewrite their daily schedule over and over again so that they really enter the data into their biocomputer. One patient rewrote her schedule eleven times. With each rewriting she found resistances coming to the surface. This exercise gave her

RETURNING TO JOY

FEAR	COUNTERSTATEMENT
I have no energy.	Of course I have no energy. I have been immobile for some time and the only way to get some energy is to move a bit. I can honor the depressed side of myself by not overly pushing myself and I can honor my health/future/potential by gentle forward movement. I look forward to a second wind and to a small degree of self-satisfaction that comes with gentle exertion.
I will embarrass myself.	I have already embarrassed myself many times in my life and yet I am still alive to tell the tale. The fear of embarrassment is actually much worse than the actual event because if I do in fact embarrass myself then I can take comfort in the fact that I was trying to improve myself. The fact is, my fear of embarrassment is part of my depression head. I can honor that fear by doing an activity that has less likelihood of causing potential embarrassment. On the other hand, I recognize that the fear of embarrassment is a manifestation of the *yetzer hara*, in a violation of the direction to disregard the judgments of anyone other than God.
I will fail.	This is not a test that one passes or fails. The idea here is to break the inertia that has developed since my depression worsened. Any step in the right direction is a victory.
It will hurt.	It will hurt and that is good. Aches and pains after physical activity, especially when it is outside my normal pattern, is a good sign. It means that my muscles have pleasantly exerted themselves. I will keep up the good work.
I don't know what to do.	Here are some examples of low impact activities that will break inertia: 1. Use the staircase instead of the elevator (or getting out a few floors earlier). 2. Park your car at the end of the parking lot. 3. Walk to shul or the *beis midrash* instead of driving.

Tackling Increased or Decreased Energy

What if I cannot do this again?	Tomorrow is another day. The destructive worry about the future is a manifestation of anxiety and depression head thinking.
I may run into someone whom I would prefer to avoid.	If this is such a major deterrent, then consider going to a place where there is little likelihood of running into this person.

the opportunity to disarm them.

Strategy 5: Set Up Your Schedule

1. Compile a list of activities that you are already accomplishing without much difficulty. Get as detailed as your recollection allows you.
2. In a second list, compile a list of activities that you would like to add to your repertoire. If you cannot think of any, speak with your therapist, your rebbe, or a trusted friend. Ask Hashem for guidance in determining what else you can do with your time.
3. Copy a number of the activity scheduling forms on the next page. Write the activities that you already perform into the appropriate time slots.
4. Fine-tune your activity schedule. Check to make sure that you have filled in as much as you can. Have you left yourself enough time to accomplish the tasks that you set for yourself? Have your overscheduled yourself? Have you neglected to plug in opportunities for physical exercise?
5. Seek the feedback of someone that you trust. Most often this will be your therapist. By seeking the in-

Day:	
12:00–2:00 A.M.	
2:00–4:00	
4:00–6:00	
6:00–8:00	
8:00–10:00	
10:00–12:00	
12:00–2:00 P.M.	
2:00–4:00	
4:00–6:00	
6:00–8:00	
8:00–10:00	
10:00–12:00	

put of someone else, you can get needed validation and support. By sharing your plans with another person, you are inherently seeking their assistance. This assistance can be as simple as someone who will follow up with you.
6. Monitor your performance and make corrections as needed. Welcome setbacks. Setbacks are part of the process of learning a new skill. If a lesson can be learned, then learn it! Write it down! Deploy the wisdom in your next attempt to set up your activity schedule.

For Those Experiencing Agitation and Agitated Energy

Agitation and agitated energy is certainly unpleasant. It is often described as "crawling within my own skin." The sensations are often accompanied by catastrophic thoughts that race through your mind. Finding comfort seems impossible.

The strategies listed below have given relief to many people. It is important to bring such symptoms to the attention of your doctor. Sometimes agitation may be a symptom of anxiety. If that is the case, your treatment may need to be adjusted to also address anxiety. In a few cases agitation may be a medication's side effect. By adjusting doses, your physician may be able to eliminate it.

In addition, these strategies are helpful in reducing even the worst agitation.

Strategy 1: Check Your Diet and Medications

Coffee and foods containing caffeine often are significant culprits in agitation. Avoid excessive consumption of such foods and beverages. Many over-the-counter remedies contain caffeine or other stimulants that may also cause agitation. Energy-boosting foods may contain caffeine, ephedra, or other kinds of stimulants. Headache remedies, cold remedies, and weight-loss preparations all contain chemicals which often act as stimulants. Speak with a pharmacist or physician if you suspect that a medication, over the counter or prescription, may be causing your agitation.

Strategy 2: Exercise

Light exercise can reduce agitation. When we exercise, beneficial chemicals are released that have a calming effect on the central nervous system. Even light exercise such as gentle walking has this effect.

Strategy 3: Rhythmic Physical Activity

Rhythmic physical activity can help restore inner calm. We are told time and again in the *Sefer HaChinuch* that our inner world is shaped by our actions. Folding laundry, doing the dishes, cleaning the car, cleaning, and organizing are a few examples of activities that can help calm you down.

Strategy 4: Record Your Thoughts

Try this exercise: Take a kitchen timer and set it for ten minutes. Take out your notebook or some blank paper. Start writing down every thought that comes into your mind. If you cannot complete writing one thought before another comes in, then leave the first one and go to the second. If the thought is significant, it will come back to you. Don't stop until the alarm goes off. If you don't feel that you have emptied out all of the thoughts swarming around your mind, then write for another ten minutes.

If you are done before the end of the ten minutes, then sit quietly and congratulate yourself for taking time out to introspect. Keep in mind the wise words of Rav Nachman of Breslov, who recommended that we all take at least one hour per day to think.

Once you have gotten your thoughts out of your mind and onto paper, determine if there is any further action to be taken. You may notice worries that need to be acted upon or discussed with others. Perhaps there is a resentment that must be put to rest through constructive dialogue. Regardless of what comes out, the mere act of getting thoughts out of your head onto paper will relax you.

Strategy 5: Sleep and Eat

Sleep deprivation and poor nutrition are usual culprits in agitation. A nap or a healthy meal may be just the right thing to help restore inner calm and comfort.

From the Author's Case Files

Barry was a fifty-two-year-old husband, father of four, and librarian. He had responded to an advertisement placed in a local newspaper by the hospital where I worked prior to my aliyah. I was running a mood-management group based on the principles in this book. The group met one evening a week. When Barry and I first met, he told me that it was good that the group was in the evening because until the late afternoon he had no energy. No matter what he did, he just could not get going.

During the course of the group, Barry learned techniques to increase his energy. He first went to his psy-

chiatrist and requested that they examine whether his medications were undermining his energy. And they were. The psychiatrist adjusted when the medication should be taken. In addition, he gave Barry another medication that served as a kind of stimulant. Barry made some diet changes and he began going for a walk every day. He and his wife or youngest daughter would take brisk walks in the park near their home. After a few months he told the group that he had never had so much energy.

Chapter 9

Tackling Problems with Concentration, Memory, and Racing Thoughts

As you have become more aware of depression, you have probably noticed that your memory and concentration have deteriorated. Carrying on a conversation or reading the newspaper is almost impossible. Your thoughts may be jumbled up as one thought vies with another for your attention. Recalling people's names may be beyond you. Seemingly simple mathematical calculations may take forever to complete. Making even the simplest of decisions evokes frustration.

These difficulties are part of your depression. Depression dulls the intellect of even the brightest among us. Perversely, problems in concentration and memory interfere with our ability to benefit from those activities that could potentially help us get out of depression, such as davening, Torah study, work, family life, and pleasurable leisure activities.

The neurobiology of depression has been blamed for deficits in concentration, decision making, and memory. But a much simpler explanation for the dullness of the depressed person can be found in the experience of depression. When you are depressed, a big part of your mind's intelligence and resources are actually quite busy. They are wrapped up in all of the negative images and destructive thinking that is part and parcel of the depression mind-set. All of this destructive mental activity means that there is less brain power for constructive uses of your mind.

What can you do about your problems with memory, decision making, and concentration? Of course, make sure to tell your mental health care provider about these problems. The good news is that with treatment of your depression, your thinking abilities will return. The following self-care strategies will help.

Strategy 1: Get Adequate Rest

Nobody can concentrate when sleep deprived. Use the sleep techniques discussed in chapter 5. If your sleep remains inadequate, speak with your health care provider. There are further tests and treatments that may be useful.

Strategy 2: Maintain a Good Diet

The mind and body are connected. It is unreasonable to expect our minds to work their best if our bodies are not in good working order. Make sure that your diet is beneficial to your brain. Ask your health care professional for help in developing a diet plan that gives you the best odds of optimal mental functioning. Some uni-

Tackling Problems with Concentration

versal steps that you can take are:

1. Have regular nutritionally balanced meals.
2. Lay off the sweets, especially when you need your mind to really be alert.
3. Avoid alcohol and other mood-altering substances.
4. Avoid heavy meals, especially when you need to focus. Heavy meals, especially those that are laden with carbohydrates and starches, usually make people feel groggy and sleepy. When your mind needs to be at its best, have small meals.

Strategy 3: Be Aware of Your Daily Rhythms

Most of us experience times of the day when we can concentrate better than at other times. For some it may be the early morning, for others it may be in the evening. You may find that the early afternoon hours are the worst times for focused activity. Try to plan heavy mental activities for when you are the most alert. Such activities include working on an important project, balancing your checkbook, or taking a course. Use those times when your brain is "slow" to do activities that don't require much concentration, such as washing the dishes or folding laundry.

Strategy 4: Develop Your Concentration Muscles

Concentration is a mental skill that can be developed with practice. Start by trying to focus on a desired topic for one minute. Consider using a kitchen timer. During the interval, focus as best you can on the material or conversation. Resolve not to answer the phone or door during this time. When the alarm goes off, take a five-minute break and celebrate the fact that you have taken the first step toward improved concentration. Repeat this cycle twenty or thirty times over a couple of days. Then expand the concentration interval to five minutes. Keep on taking those breaks. Over six to eight weeks you may be able to work yourself up to forty-five-minute intervals of focused concentration. Celebrate all success that you have in this effort.

Strategy 5: Select a Concentration-Friendly Environment

Make sure that your environment is conducive to concentration. The presence of other people, traffic, music, or the like can make concentration difficult. Choose a location that is free of any distractions. Make sure that there is adequate lighting so that you don't get eye fatigue. Try to choose a location that is bathed in bright light and is free of dark zones. Natural lighting or fluorescent lighting is the best type of light source for mental alertness. Avoid places that are uncomfortable to sit in.

Strategy 6: Ask Questions and Take Notes

Keep yourself alert by asking questions or taking notes. When attending a *shiur* or lecture, try asking yourself questions about what the speaker is saying. As difficult as it may be, ask one or two of these questions. Remember: there is no such thing as a stupid question; only stupid answers. So don't be embarrassed. Taking notes or highlighting are other ways of focusing your mind when attending a lecture or reading a book.

Strategy 7: Make Time for Worrying

Set aside a specific time each day to think about the

Tackling Problems with Concentration

things that keep entering your mind and interfering with your concentration. For example, set 4:30 to 5:00 P.M. as your worry and think time. When your mind is sidetracked into worrying during the day, remind yourself that you have a special time for worrying. The truly significant problems in our lives don't require immediate attention. Perhaps consider jotting a brief note to yourself so that you will remember to worry about it. Then let the thought go for the present, and return your focus to your immediate activity.

Strategy 8: Get More Oxygen to Your Brain!

When we sit for long periods, blood tends to pool in our lower body because of gravity. Moving around helps get the blood flowing more evenly throughout the body. As a result, more oxygen is carried to the brain and you are more alert. So get up and walk around the room for a couple of minutes. Regularly go outside and take some deep breaths of fresh air.

Strategy 9: Use Centering and Meditation Techniques

Light meditation is an excellent way to slow your brain down. One easy-to-learn method is centering. Set a timer for seven minutes. Most likely you can easily afford to take ten minutes from your life. With the exception of a literal life or death emergency, any interruption can wait seven minutes.

Lie down on the floor and get as comfortable as you can. Begin to breathe consciously. Inhale slowly and deeply so that you can see or feel your abdomen rise. Exhale slowly. Repeat the process as you gently slow your body down. Use this physical rhythm as a way to gently anchor your thoughts. By performing this exercise for five to seven minutes two to three times per day you will find that your thinking will come quickly under your control.

Strategy 10: Do Some Light, Repetitive Exercise or Activity

Sometimes you can exert some subtle control over a hyperactive mind by engaging in some light repetitive exercise or activity. Go for a slow-paced walk as you try to gently harmonize your mind with each stride. Consider folding laundry or sorting silverware. These rhythmic activities will help restore mental harmony.

Strategy 11: Seek Solitude

Another effective way to bring racing thoughts under control is to find a quiet place where you can sit in silence without the distraction. Relax and allow your mind to seek harmony with the rest of yourself.

Strategy 12: Reward Yourself

Don't forget to celebrate all your successes on the road to better concentration and alertness.

How to Improve Your Decision-Making Ability

Because of the havoc caused on your concentration and memory by your depression, you may very likely find decision making difficult. Many depressed people are so overwhelmed by decision making that they avoid taking risks of any sort. By staying with that which is familiar, they need not deal with the decision-making process. Recovery from depression lies on the other side of a decision to take risks. For this reason, the depressed person must develop decision-making abilities that support her or his efforts to find joy in life.

Why Depressed People Have Difficulty Making Decisions

For some depressed people the difficulty in making a decision is inertia and fear of pain. The actual decision appears to be clear cut. Yet fear of the pain involved in effort holds them back from taking that step.

Here is the good news, though: the depressed mind exaggerates anticipated pain. Molehills become mountains. Other people become threatening beings capable of inflicting harm. These beliefs are not reality. They are in fact the product of the depression head. Take action. You will see for yourself that the fear that holds you back from a decision is much less threatening than you thought.

Decision difficulty is also related to the fear of making a mistake. Mistakes are indeed unpleasant. They should be avoided as much as possible. However, the vast majority of mistakes are inconsequential. Your depressed mind may insist that the risk of wearing the wrong outfit or making a well-intentioned but inappropriate social comment vastly outweighs any potential benefit. Yet these mistakes are generally forgotten soon after they occur. In the grand scheme of Hashem's universe, most mistakes have absolutely no significance. To withdraw from making a decision in such inconsequential areas of life is self-sabotaging.

Certainly there are decisions in life in which the fear of making a mistake should legitimately plays a significant role. Choosing a marriage partner, buying a home, entering a seminary or yeshivah are not matters to be taken lightly. The consequences of these decisions may be lasting. How then can the depressed person make the best decision possible? Consider these decision strategies.

Strategy 1: Get Out Your Notebook

Effective decision makers use pen and paper to map out the problem, to identify possible solutions, and to keep track of how the anticipated solutions help resolve the problem. Writing information down will help you see things more clearly.

Strategy 2: Define the Decision or Problem

Problems often are not exactly the way they seem. Sitting down and defining the problem allows you the opportunity to really grasp all of its parts. A big problem can really be a group of little problems. Since smaller problems are much easier to solve than big problems, identifying them will bring you much closer to solving the big one.

Strategy 3: Brainstorm by Yourself

Once you have sufficiently broken down and defined the problem, write down some possible solutions to it. If you have identified smaller problems, then think up solutions to each of them. These solutions need not be realistic or "practical." In fact, the more you use your imagination and fantasy in this phase of problem solving, the more likely you are going to find the "right" solution.

Strategy 4: Decide on a Course of Action

Once you have thought of some solutions, choose

the best one. In choosing your course of action consider the possible difficulties involved in possible solutions that you have brainstormed. Also consider unintended consequences that may come from the possible solutions. Ideally, choose a solution that is the easiest to use and has the fewest "side effects," both in the short term and in the long term.

Strategy 5: Get Some Help from Others

Turn to others throughout the decision-making process. Avoid individuals who are dismissive of your concerns or who don't appreciate the difficulties that you are having. You need not take anyone's opinions as black and white answers to your problems. You are simply looking for some extra guidance on getting your needs met. As most people fail to ask others for help when making decisions, celebrate your efforts to do so. You are in fact following the timeless advice of Hillel in *Pirkei Avos* (2:8): the more advice, the greater is one's understanding.

From the Author's Case Files

Yocheved was a friend of a previous patient. At our first session she said that she had been depressed on and off for a number of years. Therapy had never really helped as much as medications that she had taken. She was presently mildly depressed and didn't want her depression to get worse. She hoped to make it through the winter without resuming antidepressant medications.

We met weekly for about a month and then every other week for the next five months. Yocheved was a motivated and well-educated patient. She overcame some initial shyness and embarrassment to join a dance class that I thought would help her become more active physically and socially. She made some excellent changes in her diet.

But there was one symptom that was continuing to interfere with her ability to read and write, activities that she always enjoyed, and that was the ability to focus. I gave her a handout of some of the tips presented in this chapter. She followed them. I then recommended the timer technique to her. She was a little bit leery of focusing for only one minute, but she went along with the idea. And she never looked back. I ran into her one day and she told me that her newfound ability to focus has helped her in every area of her life.

Chapter 10

Tackling Worthlessness and Guilt

All depressed people struggle with guilt and beliefs of personal worthlessness. These miserable feelings are based on exaggerations of reality. Even if there is reason for self-reproach, the guilty feelings prevent the depressed person from taking the initiative to engage in activities that would improve her or his outlook. This chapter will introduce a number of effective skills that will replace your guilt with a realistic outlook. Use them to regain power and hope in your life.

Before introducing these steps, it is first crucial to clarify some of the most confusing areas of guilt for the Torah-observant Jew.

Joy, Guilt, and Torah Observance

Continuous joyous exuberance is an emotion required for Torah observance. In fact, in the Jewish view, life is full of opportunities for rejoicing. When we take advantage of opportunities to serve Hashem even in the most seemingly insignificant way, we have opportunity to exult in well-deserved pride. After all, by exercising our free will to do any mitzvah, we generate great exaltation in Heaven.

Nevertheless, there are instances throughout a normal life when sadness and guilt, feelings quite different from joy, are necessary. Sadness and guilt evoked by the failure to follow one or more of the mitzvos is one such occasion. Halachah requires guilt and remorse be part of the *teshuvah* process. Once *teshuvah* is completed, the guilt and remorse no longer have any value. We are expected to resume the regular state of joyous exuberance normally expected by halachah.

Guilt and remorse for failing to live up to one's expectations are exactly like physical pain. Physical pain is caused by injury to the physical body. Physical pain is a signal that repair of the body is needed. It is the fear of pain that prevents us from placing our bodies in situations that pose risk of injury. Guilt and remorse are emotional pains that are evoked by violations of one's beliefs. They are emotional reactions that motivate us to change our behavior so that we are aligned with what we know to be right.

A pain sensation that occurs when there is no physical reason is a sign that the pain-sensing system has gone awry. A guilt feeling that occurs when there is no need is a symptom that something is amiss. While most of us have areas of unresolved guilt, baseless guilt is almost always a symptom of depression. It is a part of the depression mind-set of unrealistic expectations of personal perfection.

Strategies for Eliminating Baseless Guilt

Eliminating baseless guilt begins with an awareness of where you want to get to. Begin with the end in mind. For the Torah-observant Jew, the end is an absence of guilt and an overflowing sensation of your lovability to God. No matter what you have done, imagined or real, you are always welcome by Hashem. You can always come home. In the Torah view you are more beloved to Hashem than the highest-ranking heavenly angel. Your value in monetary terms exceeds all of Bill Gates or Warren Buffet's wealth.

You are a priceless treasure. Imagine the following scenarios to deepen your appreciation of your intrinsic value. While committing a terrible sin, you were caught in a fire (*chas veshalom*). In order for me to save you I would have to destroy all of the famous original works of Rembrandt. Perhaps I could only help you or remove these famous paintings from the building. Guess what. You would come out first.

Second scenario. In days of old, non-Jews would occasionally take Jews as captives. They would demand ransom knowing that Jews happily would do whatever was needed to save a captive. Let's say that they took the greatest sage of your generation as captive. Or perhaps they kidnapped a promising scientist who could conceivably provide the cure for some horrible disease. This time, however, they did not demand money. This time they demanded that you take the place of the sage or scientist. The halachah is that the community may not exchange one Jew for another, even if you were a truly wicked person. No matter what you have done, you are a priceless treasure without comparison.

Hashem's love for you is beyond anything that you can even imagine. The closest we can come to experiencing this love is to observe the loving embrace of a parent who, out of the deepest love, guides his or her daughter or son toward greater and greater levels of human development. Even if you were never blessed with such parents, this is how the prophets have told us is the love that Hashem has for each and every one of us.

Once you have come to the awareness of your overwhelming lovability, you can then dispense with feelings and thoughts of worthlessness. Even if you have intentionally violated a rule that is important to your relationship with Hashem, guilt may not be allowed to prevent you from fulfilling other mitzvos. Guilt may not be allowed to prevent you from doing *teshuvah*. Any excessive guilt or shame is a product of depression and dysfunctional thinking. Indeed, it is the *yetzer hara*.

You can further eliminate baseless feelings of guilt with these strategies.

Strategy 1: Use Opposite Action

Do things that are incompatible with your low mood and shame. Wear dressy clothing. A friend of mine sometimes wears Shabbos clothes on days when he needs to raise his self-esteem. Treat yourself to a special meal. Sing and dance, even by yourself, to *niggunim* that are energizing and uplifting.

Strategy 2: Talk to Yourself

Sit down with a piece of paper and list your sins and transgressions. Have you done *teshuvah* for them? If you have, ask yourself what you have to gain by remaining sad. Does your sadness serve any purpose?

Tackling Worthlessness and Guilt

When writing this list, you may notice that different self-statements come up. Here are two of the most common statements and their counterarguments:

STATEMENT	COUNTERARGUMENT
My transgression shows that I am a bad person.	You have committed a sin. Does that sin mean you are a sin? Why would God instruct us to do *teshuvah* if it was not understood that sins would be committed?
Why can't I ever withstand temptation?	You probably are better at withstanding temptation than you believe. Your willpower, however, may be presently too weak to stay the course when you are overwhelmed by temptation. The trick is to strengthen your willpower when the temptation is far away. Picture yourself withstanding whatever weakness you believe that you have. In the meantime, your guilt and sadness is not helping you withstand temptation, is it?

Strategy 3: Who Are Your Role Models?

We learn about guilt from significant role models in our lives such as parents, other family members, or teachers. If a significant role model accepted his or her inherent lovability and was not overly preoccupied with personal failings, chances are you may feel the same way. If, however, a significant person in your life was guilt ridden and consistently believed that he or she was unworthy, then you may also have beliefs and feelings of inadequacy.

If your feelings of guilt are based on the distorted personal view of an important role model, you can make changes in your outlook. You can choose to reject those perfectionistic beliefs and embrace a more realistic and healthy one. Look for other role models who have a balanced attitude about guilt. David HaMelech is an example of an individual who did not allow feelings of guilt to intrude on his responsibilities toward Hashem.

Strategy 4: Clarify Your Responsibility

Many people have distorted ideas about what their responsibilities are in relationships. They often think that they are responsible for how the other party feels and acts. They may also believe that in the event of some failing on their own part they should feel guilty even after they have made amends. Indeed, they may believe that they can never be forgiven.

The fact is that in any healthy relationship there must be opportunity to correct mistakes, make amends, and be forgiven. Clearly we must make adequate effort to protect the feelings and dignity of others. Once we have done so, however, their reactions are their business. They are no longer our responsibility.

Strategy 5: Make Amends

Learn how to take corrective action. Making amends will help you restore your self-confidence. You will experience a surge of dignity.

There are three essential steps to this process. The first step is to stop the negative behavior. The next step is to validate the offense as experienced by the other person. The last step is to take all of the necessary measures to ensure that you will not repeat the mistake.

Tackling Worthlessness and Guilt

Strategy 6: Freeze Errors, Lapses, and Unintended Consequences

Because of the feelings of worthlessness that destructive guilt can cause, it is advisable to ignore the guilt feelings for a little while. This way you can wait until you have recovered your ego so that you can deal effectively with guilt over personal failings or slips.

This strategy is in fact strongly recommended by Rabbeinu Yonah is his timeless work on repentance, *Shaarei Teshuvah*. Rabbeinu Yonah argues that if shame and guilt interfere with your ability to withstand temptation, then it is better to ignore the feelings and focus on change. Ultimately Hashem, our Heavenly Father, is much more interested in the actions that we take to improve ourselves. For those of us with crippling depression and guilt, that means we can skip the feelings and get on with the work.

From the Author's Case Files

> Meir was referred to me by his internist. He was a thirty-six-year-old husband and father of four. Meir worked at a large company as an accountant. He had recently gone to his internist for another refill on a prescription sleeping medication that he had started taking several months after his father passed away. The internist, realizing that the insomnia was related to depression, recommended that Meir seek some psychotherapy.
>
> Indeed, Meir was moderately depressed. He was able to work and to interact with coworkers and members of a weekly shiur that he attended. Nevertheless,

his appetite had declined and his temper had noticeably shortened. And he was having terrible insomnia that was just barely improved with the medication that the internist gave him.

Meir and I worked on addressing the symptoms that most bothered him. Within ten sessions he stated that there had been improvement in his mood and appetite. Nevertheless his sleep was poor. He spoke of how crippling thoughts and feelings of guilt would flood his mind when he put his head on his pillow. The guilt was related to the poor relationship he had had with his father. His father had not wanted Meir to become observant and was opposed to Meir's lifestyle. Needless to say, the two men became estranged and spoke little, even in the last few months of his father's life. Meir very much wanted to make amends with his father. His own anxiety about doing so caused him to put it off until there was no more time. And now Meir and I sat together figuring what he could do.

I gave Meir some reading to do. I recommended that he read Rav Yechiel Michel Tekuchinski's classic work, Gesher HaChaim. This small book helped reassure Meir that there still were repairs that could be made in their relationship. I asked him to write a list of ten ways that his father could have changed for the better. He was then to write a list of ways that he could have been a better son. We spoke about teshuvah, forgiveness, and responsibility for feelings.

During the three weeks that we worked on these issues together, Meir reported that he began to sleep better and he could take half the dose of sleep medication that he had previously. Meir eventually came to the under-

Tackling Worthlessness and Guilt

standing that both of them had made mistakes but that he was not responsible for his father's rejection of his lifestyle. Meir had made a reasonable effort to respect his father and his father was unable to grasp this.

We worked together for about four months. By the end of treatment Meir was depression free. He was sleeping much better. He had developed stronger, more positive feelings for his father. He had also made a large contribution to his children's yeshivah in memory of his father.

Chapter 11

Tackling Thoughts of Death and Suicide

The most dangerous part of depression is suicide. A severely depressed person can attempt and succeed in killing him or herself. Even if you are not severely depressed, you may likely have had fantasies that involve death or suicide. Perhaps you have wished never to wake up. You may have thought that others in your life would be better off if you were not around.

These destructive thoughts come from your depression head. Suicide is always a permanent answer to a temporary problem. Suicide is therefore always the wrong way to solve any problem. And the more you think about death, the less time and energy you have available to work on getting back into life.

What Do Thoughts about Self-Harm Mean?

Suicidal thoughts and fantasies of death almost al-

Tackling Thoughts of Death and Suicide

ways reflect the desire to stop the pain of depression. Suicidal thoughts or actions can also sometimes be misguided attempts to hurt or manipulate others. Patients often tell me about their death fantasies or suicidal actions and thoughts. I explain that they are attempting to achieve something that can be done in some more effective and less extreme way. In fact, I honor the suicidal thoughts and fantasies as a kind of emergency exit from suffering. My offer is to help my patients discover other techniques to lessen the pain and to change the people in their life.

Using Thoughts of Death to Improve Yourself

On a deeper level, suicidal thoughts and fantasies can be a gift of sorts. They remind you that you have drifted off course. They are a signal that you are in pain and that further work is needed to find alignment and fulfillment in your own life. You can use these thoughts as turning points in your life. That is wonderful news. The following strategies will help you make use of these thoughts and fantasies.

Strategy 1: Tell Someone about Your Thoughts and Fantasies

Depressions thrive on secrets. The more that you keep the darkest parts of yourself hidden from others, the more painful your depression will get. Share your thoughts of death with a trusted friend or therapist. Call a crisis hotline. Allow others to help you. The resources are out there; you must take the first step to clearly ask for them. Once you make that effort, Hashem will respond and amplify those efforts.

RETURNING TO JOY

THOUGHT	COUNTERTHOUGHT
My pain will never get better.	You may be right. You may also be wrong. Life may get better. There are countless others who have made the worst of situations into turning points in wonderful lives. You are betting the possibility of a better life on the permanence of death. That sounds like a losing wager.
My life will never get better.	It probably won't if you keep on trying to solve the problems of your life the same way that you always have. The expression "If at first you don't succeed, try, try again" is wrong. The expression should be "If at first you don't succeed, try something else." The good news is that by making small changes you can change your life for the better.
When I'm dead, I won't feel any pain.	We don't know that for sure as nobody has come back to tell us what death is like. You may find out that the hereafter is not what you expected.
They will be better off without me.	They will probably be much worse off without you. This is the case even if your relationship is strained. Family members and friends are traumatized for years after a suicide.
It will serve them right for....	If you actually die, you will not be able to enjoy the satisfaction of revenge. In fact, the greatest revenge is a life well lived. You can easily learn to get your needs met in a less self-destructive way.
What is so bad about fantasizing about death? It makes me feel better.	How about also fantasizing about how much better your life could be? You can either focus on making a life that you love or not.

Tackling Thoughts of Death and Suicide

I can get some-one's attention by overdoing, etc.	After the initial attention, the person will withdraw. He or she may be furious that you used such a severe way to get their attention. You may accidentally cause yourself great permanent harm.
I will keep these pills (or other lethal tools) around in case I need them.	Access to means of harming yourself increases your risk of intentional suicide. Give these tools of death to someone whom you trust or destroy them yourself. Then get to work on making the changes that you need to make your life better. Hashem will help you.

Strategy 2: Debate Your Dark Side

Many, many people have had thoughts of death and suicide. Very few people actually harm themselves because they debate those thoughts. For every self-destructive thought that enters their mind, several constructive thoughts can counter it. The chart above shows some of the most common dark thoughts and counters for you to consider.

Strategy 3: Take a Break

When life causes you such agony, suicide can appear to be the only thing that you have left. You feel utterly isolated and alone. Connection with another is beyond you. You have no one to turn to, to share or shoulder your burden. It is that moment that God is closest to you. He is ready to catch you. This is what King David referred to when he so achingly declared, "For my father and my mother have forsaken me, but the Lord will take me up" (*Tehillim* 27:10).

Allow yourself to rest. Go to sleep. Go to a hospital if need be. Sit in the emergency room. Give this spasm of despair an opportunity to pass. Whatever inability you have to feel His closeness is simply due to your exhaustion. When you are rested, you can resume the work of fixing your life. To give up now is to deny yourself the joy of living that could be just around the corner. As you gather your strength to make the changes in yourself and in your life that you need to make, there is tremendous *siyatta diShmaya* available to you. As the Talmud teaches, "*Haba letaher misayin oso* — He who comes to purify is helped" (*Avodah Zarah* 55a).

From the Author's Case Files

> Shoshana was waiting for me when I came in that morning. She introduced herself as I walked through the waiting room on my way to the Monday morning staff meeting. She was friendly and outgoing. She said that when she had her initial workup the week before she had heard that I would be her therapist. As I had been on vacation, I had no idea who was assigned to me. I politely excused myself as the meeting was just about to begin.
>
> What I learned about Shoshana that morning still rings in my ears. The bright and friendly twenty-nine-year-old who greeted me a few minutes earlier had just spent two weeks in the intensive care unit of our hospital. She had ingested over three hundred tablets of a well known over-the-counter pain reliever. The degree of poisoning was so high that it was a miracle that she had only minimal lasting physical or neurological injuries. Once she was medically stable she spent ten days in the inpatient psychiatric unit.
>
> This was not her first severe suicide attempt, either, nor was she a stranger to inpatient psychiatric care.

Tackling Thoughts of Death and Suicide

Since her junior year of high school, Shoshana had a virulent form of psychotic depression. And now I was to be entrusted with helping her stay alive, stay out of the hospital, and make a life for herself. I knew that I didn't have the luxury of time, given how lethal Shoshana's suicide attempts were getting. I knew that the risk of successful suicide goes up with each attempted suicide. Frankly, despite my training and my experience I was nervous. I also knew that I was literally engaged in saving a life and I could count on siyatta diShmaya.

The two of us got to work. Following the guidelines of cognitive therapy, we focused on mapping out a life that she wanted so that the option of leaving it would be less compelling. We focused on what she wanted to live for instead of on why she wanted to die. I correctly assumed that her previous well-meaning therapists had focused on stopping her from dying; I thought that we would succeed by focusing on how to live.

Because she had been out of life, so to speak, for so many years, Shoshana really had no goals. In one of her lengthy hospitalizations she had successfully passed her Graduate Equivalency Diploma (GED) exam. She was therefore officially a high school graduate. But where to from there? I gave her some goal-setting forms that another patient and I had developed together. Shoshana was asked to fill them out over the course of a week. I also arranged for her to meet with an occupational therapist who could assess her vocational strengths and abilities. Within a month, she began taking her first course in creative writing at the local community college. When I last heard from her, she was completing her associate's degree in education.

Throughout her therapy we spoke often and honestly about her suicidal thoughts and impulses. Instead of fighting them, I befriended and honored them. These impulses came from a part of Shoshana that wanted to save her from agonizing pain. They were an escape hatch that she desperately needed to carry on. Shoshana agreed to focus on two goals: setting up other escape hatches and reducing that pain. With all of the anger that Shoshana had created in her family over the years and all of the pain that she had caused herself, there was a lot of work to do. We met twice a week for eighteen months. The going was hard and filled with setbacks. But there were no suicide attempts during this period. Most important, Shoshana was able to get a momentum of success that keeps her going to this day.

I would like to think that it was my exceptional abilities as a therapist that are responsible for this miracle. Perhaps to some degree it was. But I followed the treatment protocols of cognitive therapy to the letter, so maybe it was that which helped. My supervisor and colleagues all gave me excellent feedback and guidance throughout the therapy. While in treatment Shoshana was started on a new medication that appears to have helped as well. Maybe it was my stubborn belief in her. Maybe it was simply the fact that she had the opportunity to start all over again in an environment that celebrated what she could do and did not fight with her over what she couldn't. Whatever it was, Shoshana has made great use of these resources. When I left the hospital to make aliyah, our separation was bittersweet. She taught me so much about human potential, and I will always be grateful to her for that.

Chapter 12
Tackling Irritability and Anger

Depressed people often feel angry and irritable. Minor irritations that went unnoticed before can now become major aggravations. You find that you are in an almost constant state of irritability. Whereas you were once flexible in your relationships, you may have become much more rigid. Or you may have adopted a passive, "I don't care" attitude because others do not measure up.

The good news is that you can change. Even the most irritable, anger-filled people have learned to respond to the world in a freer, more joy-filled way. The following strategies will get you started replacing your irritability with tolerance and compassion.

Strategy 1: Make Serenity and Kindness More Important than Convenience and Comfort

We choose how to respond to events in our lives based on priorities. Imagine being in the White House and accidentally tearing your pants. Would you start carrying on? Most likely you wouldn't. This is because you have made decorum a greater priority than self-expression. By making serenity a priority over comfort, gratification, or status, you will find that you can handle rude behavior, frustration, and inconvenience without going to pieces.

In fact, when you choose to put aside your own agenda by choosing serenity over gratification, you are doing a number of mitzvos. You are physically demonstrating your faith in Hashem by surrendering your will to His will. You are refining your *middos*. By refraining from anger, you are avoiding idol worship. By showing kindness, you are following in the ways of Hashem. And by avoiding anger, an emotion that can be so damaging to your physical health, you are fulfilling the mitzvah of caring for your health.

Strategy 2: Clarify Your Beliefs about Anger

The myths about anger abound. See the chart on the facing page for some examples.

Strategy 3: Tune in to Your Self-Talk

We all carry on constant dialogues with ourselves throughout our every waking moment. *Hmm…should I have the blueberry cheesecake or stick with the low-fat chocolate parfait?* or *Did that guy just look at me or was he looking at someone else?* are just two examples of those silent conversations that we have with ourselves. When we experience anger, we have conversations that contain information about how we are being affected by events around us. Whether we are aware or not, these conversations are going on well before we hit the boiling point. By tuning in to our self-statements we can avoid anger because we can take corrective action before we go nuclear.

Tackling Irritability and Anger

MYTH	REALITY
Anger is bad.	Like all emotions, it all depends on what you do with it. Anger can be harnessed for great good in your life. It can also destroy your life and the lives of the people around you.
Venting anger is a good way of dealing with it.	Yes and no. It can be helpful to get your anger off your chest, whether you do it by telling a friend about it, venting to your therapist, or writing about it in your journal. The problem, though, is when you stop with venting and fail to address the issue that evoked the anger in the first place. Most people spend countless hours of their lives spewing forth their anger in a form of verbal diarrhea. The "catharsis" seems to give them the illusion that they are doing something constructive with their anger. What a waste.
It's good to get all your anger out.	A number of recent studies indicate that people who let their anger burst forth are at risk for all sorts of medical problems, such as heart disease and high blood pressure. The same studies found that people who manage their anger with many of the techniques listed here live healthier lives, are more likely to enjoy satisfying relationships, and seem to have happier lives.

Strategy 4: Know Your Warning Signs

Anger does not just happen. We don't just explode, sulk, or throttle out of the blue. Angry behaviors are the end point of a complex process of perception, processing, evaluation, and execution. Most likely, anger responses have been going on well before you did anything about them. Perhaps your hands clenched up, you turned sideways to the person provoking you, or you found yourself crossing your arms over your chest. Awareness of these warning signs gives you options besides falling back on ineffective anger patterns. You can remove yourself from the situation, do deep breathing exercises, set limits on what you will tolerate, or use some other coping technique.

Common anger warning signs are:

- Increased heartbeat
- Sweating
- Tingling sensations on the back of the neck
- Fidgeting
- Feelings of impatience

Strategy 5: Identify Your Fears

Anger is often a cover for fear. Anger is related to "fight or flight response." When threatened, humans respond with the drive to protect themselves or run away. This response is effective when we are confronted by criminals. When we are stood up by a friend or our child breaks a cherished piece of art, the "fight or flight" response is less helpful. So when you find yourself seething in anger, ask yourself, *What am I so afraid of?* Most likely it's an irrational fear.

The confusion between fear and anger is a particular problem for men. Because boys are often encouraged to be aggressive when threatened, they grow up into men who automatically respond with anger to any sort of

Tackling Irritability and Anger

threat. The Torah-observant man must therefore work especially hard on monitoring his anger. By being accurately aware of his feelings, he can more effectively get his needs met.

Strategy 6: What Spices Are You Adding?

You learned about cognitive spices that depressed people add to adversity in chapter 7. What spices are you adding that leave you feeling angry and frustrated? Are you catastrophizing minor inconveniences? Are you jumping to conclusions that a trivial difficulty is in fact a major setback?

Strategy 7: Honor Your Anger

Anger is a helper. It has been the force behind the great social revolutions in human history. It can be the force behind making important changes in your life. When you find yourself getting angry, introspect. Look to see what the feeling is trying to tell you. Perhaps the anger is in response to an imbalance of power in a relationship. It can also be a sign that your expectations in a given situation are not being met. This information can help you do something about the problem.

Strategy 8: Learn to Be Assertive

Many people who have difficulty with anger are the meekest people you have ever met. They don't want to "make waves," so they let others take advantage of them. The problem with this is obvious. They often seethe internally and spend their sleepless nights ruminating about how they wish they could get back at whoever or whatever has slighted them. They may even explode in a spectacular nuclear detonation. All because they didn't know how to assert themselves in a humane and self-respectful manner. If this pattern fits you, learn how to be assertive.

Strategy 9: Develop Anger Flexibility

No kind of anger response is always the right one. So be flexible. When it comes to anger, there are few hard-and-fast rules. There will even be times that yelling is appropriate, just as there are times when ignoring a provocation is the right way to go.

The point is that our anger responses should not always be the same. People who have difficulty with anger almost always get angry the same way regardless of the trigger. They yell and curse or sulk whether a friend has stood them up or someone cuts them in line at the supermarket.

Strategy 10: Examine Your Anger Role Models.

All of us have images of how we should or should not express our anger. Perhaps we grew up in a home where our parents carried on with unbridled anger and tantrums. Conversely, perhaps our parents never expressed any form of anger. Or perhaps we find ourselves referencing back to our favorite celebrity and how we imagine he or she responds to provocation.

Awareness of your references and role models allows you to objectively appraise their ability to deal with anger. Perhaps Dad's tantrums or Mom's sulking were not really that effective. Just because they did it doesn't mean that you have to. Choose a new role model for the expression of anger or assertiveness.

Tackling Irritability and Anger

Strategy 11: Be Patient with Your Anger

Anger management takes work. No matter what anybody says or writes, anger is not an easy emotion to master. By the time that you read these passages, you will have developed ingrained anger habit patterns that generate automatic anger responses. Any effort that you plan to make on improving the way you deal with anger is going to take some work and time. Don't expect overnight transformations. Instead, focus on making one small alteration in your anger repertoire at a time.

Strategy 12: Get Assistance for Areas of Chronic Anger

The anger management techniques that you are reading about here (or in any self-help material) will most likely not be sufficient to help you deal with long-term anger. Such anger, usually related to traumatic events and destructive relationships, will best be dealt with in therapy. On the other hand, using these techniques for "normal" anger will help you with "major" anger issues because you will be able to use some of these techniques for some of the little parts of the big issues.

From the Author's Case Files

> *I met Dovid through a colleague of mine who had been doing family therapy with Dovid and his wife and children. The family had sought treatment because of the frequent angry outbursts of the two oldest children. During the family therapy sessions it became clear that Dovid also had some difficulty with anger. My colleague pointed out to Dovid that unless he got his own*

anger under control his children would not make any changes. Dovid agreed and he came to see me.

Dovid told me about his difficulties with anger. He told me how guilty he felt afterwards. He saw his angry outbursts as violating his values as a Jew and recognized that his tirades were damaging to his family. But he believed himself powerless to stop.

When asked about his mood, Dovid told me that he was not particularly happy with his job. He was a supervisor at a municipal agency, and his new supervisor had him baffled by inconsistent demands. His greatest disappointment, however, came from his turbulent home life.

He took it as no surprise when I told him that I believed he was mildly depressed. When I explained that his anger and depression were interrelated, he knew at once what I was talking about. "I know that I am too hard on my son and that I am way too hard on myself. But how can I stop? I don't know how to get Shlomo [his son] to study and I have had it up here [pointing to his neck] with all of the fighting. Sometimes it seems that screaming at him is the only way to get his attention."

That first session concluded with some homework assignments. Dovid told me that he enjoyed reading and studying history, so the first assignment was to think of two instances in which conflict was averted through diplomacy and then two conflicts where diplomacy failed. He was then asked to keep an unanger log in which he would record twenty instances in which he didn't get angry or lash out. While he said that he understood the purpose of the first assignment, he was confused by the second assignment. I told him that it would all become clear next time we met.

Our next session took place one week later. Dovid gave me a brief history lesson. He commented that is was too bad that the countries who decided to go to war could not wait a bit longer because in the interim their adversaries would have collapsed on their own. In that observation we discovered that time was almost always a factor in his anger. He simply wanted his children to behave or change immediately. He recognized that if he was willing to have some more patience he would find that he didn't have to yell.

We then examined his unanger list. On it were numerous times when he had remained calm and focused. When I asked him how he remained calm when his son came late to shul, he said that he had become engrossed in a new sefer that he had brought with him. When I asked him how he ignored his wife's slow departure from a wedding, he said that he stepped outside and admired the grounds of the wedding hall.

Despite his earlier confusion about this assignment, he quickly understood that I was trying to get him to see firsthand that when it came to provocation he had choices. He could choose peace and forgiveness or simply to ignore the irritating behavior of people whom he loved. Seeing his successes enabled him to find other ways to curb his anger. Most importantly, he was able to become a positive role model for his children.

Chapter 13

Shame, Modesty, and Self-Esteem

Shame is one of the most disabling emotions of depression. Excessive shame sabotages our ability recover from our depression. We think ourselves unworthy of the positive steps that would restore our self-confidence. Fearful of losing the little dignity that we might perceive, we withdraw from taking even the slightest risks.

For the Torah-observant Jew, however, shame can be even more complex. On one hand, shame and modesty are character traits that are praised throughout Torah literature. On the other hand, we all know firsthand how shame is such a destructive leash on our ability to grow. This shame is twofold. There is the shame inherent in depression. And there is the embarrassment that we are in need of treatment.

The Difference between Healthy Shame and Dysfunctional Shame

How can you distinguish between shame encouraged by *mussar* books and the shame of depression? The

Shame, Modesty, and Self-Esteem

answer is easier than you might think. The shame and modesty extolled in the Torah is compatible with productive and constructive activity. The shame of depression smothers and strangles you into deeper and deeper passivity.

Healthy shame is an aspect of gratitude to Hashem for one's talents, gifts, and achievements. In order to have healthy shame, one is in fact aware of these talents, gifts, and achievements, hardly the state of mind when one is ashamed of her or his very existence. Dysfunctional shame prevents you from serving Hashem and helping others.

If you believe that you have excessive shame, the following strategies will help. Be gentle and patient with yourself. You very likely have felt excessive shame long enough for it to be second nature. Apply these strategies with long-term improvement in mind.

Strategy 1: Become Aware of Your Shame in All Its Details

Measure your shame. Shame can exist at the very core of one's being. Therefore, the shamed person is unaware of how shame filters into everything he or she does. To help you identify the areas of your life where you may be affected by shame, consider the following list of daily activities.

1. Introducing yourself to others
2. Starting a conversation
3. Calling up an acquaintance just to chat
4. Saying no to someone else's request for help or for a favor
5. Asserting your rights

6. Giving someone a compliment
7. Acknowledging that you made a mistake
8. Asking for assistance from a friend, family member, or acquaintance
9. Asking for a raise
10. Asking for assistance from your boss or coworker(s)
11. Saying no to a request to work extra at the expense of your needs or convenience or without added compensation
12. Putting up with harassment including abusive, derisive, or discriminatory behavior

If you have difficulty in any of these activities, then excessive shame may be one of the causes. By improving yourself in any of these activities, you will challenge and weaken the shame that holds you back.

Strategy 2: Challenge Your Erroneous Beliefs about Mistakes

Accept your intrinsic worth. The healing from shame begins when we can begin to embrace the belief that each person belongs to the human race, that no person is totally shameful, bad, or perfect. We are all "works in progress." We are not charged with being perfect, but rather with making the best decisions and taking the best actions that we can. Mistakes and errors in judgment are simply indications that we were not aware of the total picture before we made a decision or took the action. We can learn from our mistakes and resolve to do better next time.

Shame, Modesty, and Self-Esteem

Strategy 3: Imagine Living without Shame

Think about your intrinsic beauty and worth. How does Hashem really look at you? He looks at you with love, just the way that a parent might look at his or her child. Next, imagine yourself living your life without the shackles of shame. How would your relationships change? How would your whole life change? What things would you do? How would you feel?

Strategy 4: Set Positive Goals

Actions and behaviors have the strongest influence over our mental attitudes. Unless you live your life proudly, you will still feel shackled by shame. Celebrate every victory against shame-based thinking. When you assert yourself or allow yourself to experience some pleasure, validate yourself. Spread the good news to your supporters. You can break the chains of shame link by link and build a self that is brimming with hope, dignity, and confidence, one small action at a time.

Strategy 5: Help Others See the Beauty in Themselves

Teach what you want to learn. This is especially true in overcoming shame. We can fight our own shame by helping others — friends, coworkers, and family members — overcome theirs.

Strategy 6: Change How You Treat Yourself

Choose to love yourself. Love and acceptance are the greatest enemies of shame. You cannot count on unconditional love from anyone except yourself, so say these words out loud and say them often: "I love myself and I accept myself exactly as I am, right now, at this moment." Even if you don't believe these words yet, say them anyway.

Life without dysfunctional shame is not a license for self-indulgence. Life without shame, however, is about serving Hashem in joy. When you are unshackled by shame, you have the energy that you need to do mitzvos with a full heart.

Strategy 7: Heal the Wounds of Childhood

Healing shame often involves dealing with the wounds of childhood. Connecting areas of difficulty in adulthood with something in one's childhood will help you break free of the shame in adulthood. For example, if you find that you have poor body image as an adult, look back into the messages that you received about your body as a child. If you have difficulty accepting yourself when you make a mistake, consider messages that you received as a child when you did something less than perfect.

While exploring one's childhood can be helpful, there are two hazards to be aware of. The first is that many people who get overly involved in resolving their shame by examining their childhoods often get so caught up in blaming their families that they fail to address what they can do to improve their lives *now*. Blaming others for one's problems is always destructive. Blame strengthens the belief that forces outside of ourselves control our destiny.

The second danger in blaming our families for our shame and difficulties in our adulthood is that we often fail to recognize that our parents and family members almost always experienced the same amount of shame that we do now. Blaming them or trying to make them change or apologize will only generate more pain for you. Instead, teach by example. Live your life as an adult without shame and without low self-esteem.

From the Author's Case Files

Noam and I played telephone tag for three days. Having to call people back many times is not something terribly uncommon, but it later became clear that those missed phone calls were caused by the all-too-familiar deep-seated shame of depression. You see, each time I called and got Noam's answering machine he heard me leave a message. And he struggled with whether to accept the offer of assistance or to withdraw into his cocoon. Baruch Hashem, Noam ultimately made the right choice.

We quickly got down to work. He and I examined his symptoms and strategized ways to reduce them. Once he was able to go back to work and college we began to explore some of the psychological causes for his depression and anxiety.

Without a doubt, shame was the theme music that ran through Noam's life. Despite excellent grades in school and a sterling work record, Noam was utterly embarrassed of himself. He was convinced that he was worthless and an embarrassment to his family. He easily dismissed his accomplishments as things that anybody could do.

It took a lot of work for Noam to begin to question the accuracy of his shame. At first he dismissed every single one of my counterarguments to his underlying belief. I actually thought for a couple of sessions that Noam was going to stop therapy.

But then a miracle happened. As part of his college

studies, Noam decided to write an article about the Nazi treatment of the disabled during the Holocaust. He researched the horrors visited by the Nazis and learned that in Germany, one's right to life was based only on one's ability to work. He contrasted this despicable attitude with the Torah concept that all people are created in the image of Hashem. And that included him.

When he came in for his regular session I noticed that his face was a bit brighter. His step was a bit more confident. I asked about it. He told me about his paper and that he realized that maybe he was being too hard on himself. Even if he had not accomplished everything that he wanted, he was still a child of Hashem, a relative of Avraham Avinu.

With that he was ready to take on his shame. He practiced the techniques that I taught him. He said no to destructive thoughts. He developed pride in his accomplishments, recognizing that each one was an opportunity to sanctify Hashem's name in this world.

Noam is now married. I ran into him at a wedding recently. He looked great and sounded terrific. And to think that just a few years earlier he couldn't see anything good in himself. I am grateful to Hashem that I got a chance to help such a fine young man find the truth about himself.

Chapter 14

Reducing Anxiety

Depressions don't occur in a vacuum. Most of us, when we are clinically depressed, also experience dysfunctional anxiety. No discussion of clinical depression would be complete without some essential information on anxiety.

Anxiety is associated with fear. However, that is only part of the definition. Anxiety is an experience that involves our thoughts, feelings, and physiology. The more anxious we are, the more anxiety affects everything about us. The feeling most commonly connected with anxiety is fear. You may also experience dread, terror, or panic. In some ways feelings of laziness, boredom, and tiredness can be emotions that are linked to anxiety. From a health perspective, anxiety exacts a great toll on the body. People experiencing anxiety usually have higher than optimal blood pressure. Digestive ailments, sleep problems, and aches and pains are all manifestations of anxiety.

When we are anxious, our thinking is filled with thoughts of dread. Our thoughts are focused on the perceived dangers. Avoiding the feared event is the only possible way to reduce this terror. When anxiety increases to this level of panic, hypervigilance takes over. In a state of hypervigilance we are profoundly focused, scanning the environment for impending danger. All we see is information that further confirms the perception of danger.

The relationship between anxiety and depression is not coincidental. Many of depressed adults report long periods of anxiety before they became depressed. This unremitting, low-grade anxiety often becomes the breeding ground for the passivity of depression.

Good and Bad Anxiety

One might wonder if all anxiety is bad. The Master of the Universe, however, blessed us with anxiety so that we would protect ourselves from real physical, social, and spiritual dangers. Protective anxiety is therefore a great blessing.

Excessive and baseless anxiety, however, is not life protecting or life enhancing; it is life limiting. It is this kind of anxiety that is often experienced by the depressed person. In order to break free of your depression, you will want to learn to deescalate this anxiety. The following strategies will give you the basic tools that you need to move forward.

Strategy 1: Measure Your Anxiety

Managing anxiety starts with awareness of it. Begin with measuring it. Here is a list of the most common symptoms of dysfunctional anxiety.

- Difficulty breathing

Reducing Anxiety

- Dizziness
- Faintness
- Fear of being alone
- Fear of dying
- Fear of losing control
- Fear of the worst happening
- Feeling hot
- Feelings of choking
- Flushed face
- Fright
- Hands trembling
- Heart pounding or racing
- Inability to relax
- Indigestion or discomfort in abdomen
- Lightheadedness
- Nausea
- Nervousness
- Numbness or tingling
- Shakiness
- Sweating (not due to heat)
- Unsteadiness

Which symptoms do you feel most? When do you

experience them most often? Share this information with your mental health professional.

Strategy 2: Dismiss the Utility of Dysfunctional Anxiety

There is nothing helpful about panic. Highly anxious businessmen make poor business decisions. Highly anxious parents make poor parenting choices. If you have chronic dysfunctional anxiety, then you may falsely believe that anxiety is the key to survival. The problem with this assumption is the fact that when you are so anxious you can easily make poor choices. In an effort to reduce your anxiety, you may take the easiest action. Sometimes the easiest action may in fact be the worst choice.

Strategy 3: Debate Your Anxious Thoughts

Anxiety is the response that you get when you perceive the demands of a situation exceed your resources. When anxious, the dialogue between your mind and body focuses on this deficit.

In the average person's life there are very little real threats. Believe it or not, we have many more abilities to take on the demands of day-to-day living than we imagine. We have successfully dealt with similar situations in the past. We have what it takes to get through a threatening situation. Best of all, we have Hashem on our side, helping us along.

You can easily reduce your anxiety by taking the time to counter your distorted perceptions. Begin this by listing your anxious thoughts. Each thought may have another thought associated with it. By gentle probing you can uncover your dominant fears. Once in the pos-

Reducing Anxiety

session of this information you can begin to explain to yourself why you have much less to fear than you originally believed.

Many patients find the completion of an anxiety-reducing form to be helpful. Here is an example of one such form.

Present physical sensations and feelings	
Desired physical sensations and feelings	
Perceived needs causing anxiety	
Resources already in your possession	
Concrete plans to get needed resources	

Completing the form is straightforward. The goal is to achieve feelings of peace and calmness. All problems can be better solved when you are calm and relaxed. Use the list of anxiety symptoms above to complete row 1. List some of the feelings that you would like to have. The feeling list in appendix A should be consulted. The remaining rows require you to take a step back to look objectively at your perceptions and what you need to do in order to solve the problem.

Strategy 4: Get Physical

Exercise is one of the best anxiety busters known. Moderate exercise can immediately drop your level of anxiety. Exercise helps restore a pleasant feeling of serenity. Going for an walk, using a treadmill, and swimming are just a few examples of the kinds of exercise that have antianxiety effects. Once you feel relaxed, you can then return to whatever was triggering the anxiety with a calm and clear mind.

Medications, Alcohol, Food, and Anxiety

When excessive anxiety interferes in one's life, medication is often turned to for relief. Medication has an excellent track record for reducing anxiety and restoring calm. The most common medication prescribed for the reduction of anxiety is Diazepam or Valium and its derivatives. Those include Xanax, Ativan, and Klonopin.

Despite their effectiveness, there are three significant drawbacks to the use of these medications.

- They all cause sleepiness, which usually interferes with one's ability to function.
- They are all highly addictive.
- They offer nothing in the way of preventing excessive anxiety in the future.

In recent years, neuroscientists have found that many of the commonly prescribed antidepressants have antianxiety benefits as well. These medications are nonaddictive and usually are not sedating.

Unfortunately, many individuals who suffer from excessive anxiety turn to alcohol for relief. While alcohol can provide a brief respite from anxiety and panic, it always comes with a great price. Dependence on alcohol and illicit drugs leads to physical disease, family breakdown, unemployment, and actions that have lasting and devastating effects on oneself and on society.

Excessive consumption of food is another way that many people try to reduce their anxiety. Indulging in comfort food is certainly understandable. Unrestrained consumption, however, can have far-ranging negative physical and psychological consequences. However, perhaps the greatest drawback to using alcohol, drugs, or food is the fact that one never has the opportunity to eliminate the cause of the anxiety. These forms of self-medication all backfire, usually in the grimmest of ways.

Emergency Anxiety Reducers

If you have had difficulty with anxiety or have experienced panic attacks, it's a good idea to have some first aid available. The following is a list eleven things you can do now to reclaim your serenity.

1. Take ten cleansing breaths.
2. Eat a healthy snack.
3. Take a nap or simply stare out the window for ten minutes. Let your thoughts flow through you. There is no need to act on anything now. Anything that is truly important will come back to you when you need it.
4. Lie on the ground for ten minutes.
5. Doodle or scribble in your recovery notebook for five minutes.
6. Go for a ten-minute walk, regardless of the weather or time of day
7. Set a clock and light a candle. Watch the candle flicker for eight minutes; write thoughts that go through your mind on a piece of paper.

8. Listen to classical music and conduct as you listen.
9. Read inspirational literature of your choice.
10. Write out your thoughts in your log until you feel yourself grounded and focused
11. Brainstorm. Write down twenty small things you can do to resolve the problem. Five of the twenty must include ridiculous solutions.

From the Author's Case Files

Bat Sheva was referred to me by a relative with whom I had worked several years before. Bat Sheva, a thirty-six-year-old woman and mother of four children, had moved into the area about a year earlier when her husband was transferred by his employer. She insisted that she had no reason to feel so miserable because her home life was good. Her children had adjusted to their new community and schools. Her husband had gotten a promotion which increased their income and also allowed him to be at home more often.

Still, Bat Sheva was in agony. She confided to me that she was a nervous wreck. She could hardly sleep at night and only with the assistance of some over-the-counter sedative. She felt uncomfortable inside her own skin. When she encountered other people, for example when she picked up her children from school or when she went shopping, she felt one step away from falling apart. The more her veneer of self-assuredness dissolved, the more I could feel this poor woman's abject terror.

In the course of the workup, Bat Sheva told me that

Reducing Anxiety

she had often felt anxious. Until her relocation she had always had the familiar surroundings of her hometown and family to support her. Now that was gone.

Because it had been some time since she felt comfortable, I decided to help her reconnect with positive feelings. With some encouragement, she visualized a time in the past when she felt calm and powerful. When I asked her what event that was, she told me that she had gone for a hike with some friends right before she had gotten married. She told me how beautiful the woods were. The sounds and smells were so vivid. She recounted how long they had walked until they got to a beautiful meadow overlooking a valley that opened before them. She described feeling on top of the world and being at peace with herself. I told her to savor that memory as long and as deeply as she wished.

When Bat Sheva emerged from this exercise she was visibly changed. There was more color in her face. Her body was relaxed and her breathing regular and comfortable. She smiled and said that she hadn't felt so good in a long time.

From that fifteen-minute exercise we developed a plan that ultimately helped her regain her serenity and calmness. Bat Sheva joined a local women's meditation group and made time to exercise outdoors. She quickly learned that her anxiety and worries were manageable. She could challenge her anxious thoughts and sensations.

Chapter 15

Staying on Course

Depressions end. Using the strategies of this book you have beaten the symptoms of depression into remission. Good job! And the even better news is that the work is not yet over. Why is this good news? Because depressions frequently reoccur, but you can take continuous preventative steps to avoid relapse. Relapse prevention works! And that is great news.

Relapse prevention is important for everyone who has been depressed. Nevertheless, it is especially important for certain types of people. Examples of individuals who are especially vulnerable for relapse include:

- Those who have moved, switched jobs, experienced the loss of a loved one, married, had a child, or experienced any significant life change.

- Those whose sleep problems never improved significantly even while in active treatment for their depression.

- Individuals who have had previous episodes of depression.

- Those with chronic disease.

Staying on Course

While these individuals are at significant risk of becoming depressed again, everyone is vulnerable. The following strategies will keep you on the road of recovery.

Strategy 1: Keep Mental Health Checkups

For those who are serious about remaining depression free, mental health checkups are essential. A regular biannual meeting with your mental health professional can help you monitor your emotional health. In such sessions you can review the progress that you are making in your life. Your therapist can help you examine areas of stress in your life. He or she can help you see to it that you are adequately caring for yourself.

Strategy 2: Keep Taking Your Medications

Just as medication may have been helpful in relieving symptoms of depression, it is effective in preventing relapse. Continue taking them as directed by your health care provider. In most cases you and your physician may lower the dose of medication that you are taking. The benefits of a maintenance level of medication are twofold: 1) it seems to provide a psychological shock absorber so that you are not as easily overwhelmed by stress, and 2) it shortens your response time to a regular dose of antidepressant medication if you need to resume it.

Will you always need to take medication? To be honest, nobody really knows. Antidepressant medications have been shown time and again to be safe even when taken for years. There are certainly many medical conditions that require the use of medication throughout one's life span. High blood pressure is an example of one such disease. Nevertheless, you and your health care provider may decide to experiment with stopping your medication.

Strategy 3: Keep Using Those Strategies!

The strategies described in *Returning to Joy* that helped you relieve the symptoms of depression will also help you prevent relapses. Monitoring your mood and how you are spicing the events of your life are especially helpful. Regular exercise and a nutritious dietary regimen should form the backbone of your antirelapse plan. Continue focusing on setting and accomplishing goals.

Strategy 4: Watch Out for "Out of Control" Stress

It is not uncommon for adults to plunge back into their previous stress-filled lives after beating back their depressions. Unfortunately they quickly learn something that they forgot to learn the first time: out-of-control stress makes people depressed and miserable. There is nothing wrong with occasionally taking on excessive responsibility such as helping out with a yeshivah fund-raising campaign or other *chesed* project. However, when you are finding that you are consistently unable to relax because of too many obligations, you are overdoing it. Your schedule should allow for ample sleep, exercise, healthy meals, and enjoyable social activities. Anything less is a prescription for relapse.

Strategy 5: Be Aware of Difficult Periods of the Year

Individuals who have had previous depression are often vulnerable to a Seasonal Affective Disorder (SAD). With the onset of winter, usually after Sukkos when the clocks are changed, many people notice a deterioration in their mood. This phenomenon is related to the lack of sunlight and the tendency to remain indoors.

Because of this vulnerability, it is important to monitor the ups and downs of your mood as summer and fall give way to winter. Psychiatrists often recommend an increase in the dose of antidepressant medication to counter this vulnerability. Many people have also found some relief in the use of a specially designed electric light. This device comes very close to duplicating the full spectrum of light rays emitted by the summer sun. Most lighting stores carry them.

Yartzeits and sad times of the Jewish year can also stoke your vulnerability to mild relapse. You are not alone in the low moods that you may encounter. Many patients have shared with me that the period prior to a *yartzeit* is most difficult. It is especially important to reach out to others for support during such a time.

Strategy 6: Keep Winners in Your Life

The people whom you associate with are vital to your personal success. This includes your success at keeping depression at bay. Depressed, passive, and angry people will destroy the positive energy that you have developed in your recovery. Optimistic, joyous people will keep you on track. Make sure that you have some contact with such people every day. Contact can be as brief as a phone call or e-mail. Even better is setting up learning sessions with such people. Socialize with them. Attend shul with them. They will help you keep your priorities straight.

Strategy 7: Recommit Yourself to Torah and Mitzvos

Hashem graced us with Torah and mitzvos for our

benefit. This includes our physical and mental health. The mitzvos help us stay focused on what is truly important in life. That alone has a powerful ability to prevent depression relapse. This does not mean that you need to radically change yourself all at once. It does not mean that you must try to form yourself into someone that you are not. What it does mean is that prayer, learning, *tzedakah*, and *chesed* should become a more integral part of who you are.

Depression and Our Lives

Chapter 16

Depression in the Observant Family

Relationships are not immune to the destructive effects of depression. This is especially so in family relationships. Family members are often the first ones to confront a loved one about depression. Family members must often assume some responsibilities for the depressed person. And, of course, family members may correctly or incorrectly hold themselves responsible for their loved one's depression.

Patients and family members must therefore be aware of how depression affects relationships. Family members will find it helpful to read this and other books on depression and its treatment. It is usually helpful for the depressed person's therapist to hold periodic family meetings to discuss family-related factors in the recovery process. Quite frequently it is recommended that family members pursue their own treatment.

The following sections are devoted to the family relationships most commonly affected by depression. However, every family is unique and few general principles can be articulated. The reader is therefore urged to discuss special concerns with his or her psychotherapist.

Parents of the Depressed Adult

Nothing frightens a parent more than a child's illness. This is the case even if the child has a family of her or his own. The possibility that a child may not only be ill but also have a psychiatric illness such as clinical depression is doubly terrifying. This is especially the case in the Torah-observant families, where achievement and conformity are such central values.

Parental fear can unfortunately lie at the core of common counterproductive responses. Parents often respond with denial to their son or daughter's difficulties, social withdrawal, and other symptoms. Parents may say the most hated words a depressed person ever hears, "Just snap out of it!" Parents may react with alarm when their child must take a hiatus from dating or work because of depression. The child's efforts at recovery may be belittled. This shame, fear, and anger can drive a wedge between the child and parent just at the time when the child needs his or her parents.

So how should a parent respond to a child's depression? Encouragement and acceptance are the best places to start. You cannot take the place of a professional, but you can encourage your child. You can gently dispute the negative thoughts filling her or his mind. You can provide an environment that is conducive to recovery by deflecting the curiosity of relatives and friends. You can gently nudge your child to experiment with activities that may alleviate symptoms. Most important, you serve as a cheerleader in their recovery.

Unconditional acceptance and belief in your child's future helps immeasurably. When your child knows that he or she is loved unconditionally, he or she will be ready to share other ways that you can be of help. Seek the assistance of a knowledgeable rabbi or competent psychotherapist if you believe that further guidance is needed. If your son or daughter invites you, attend joint sessions with your child's psychotherapist.

Your son or daughter's depression may exacerbate already difficult areas of your relationship. Conflict may arise as to whether parents are responsible for their child's depression. These very wrenching issues must be addressed with a competent mental health professional.

The Spouse of the Depressed Adult

As difficult as it is for the depressed person, in many ways it is even more difficult for the spouse. Judging by appearances, the depressed spouse looks like he or she can fulfill all of his or her regular responsibilities. But you know all too well that looks are deceiving. The prying and judging eyes of family members, neighbors, and coworkers don't make it any easier. You may have found yourself having to carry on appearances despite the increasing incapacities of your spouse.

The word that therapists hear most often from the spouses of depressed people is "exhausted." The next most common words are ashamed, confused, and angry. All of these feelings are valid and understandable. As your wife or husband has become incapacitated, you may have shouldered more and more. Just as you have taken care of one pressing need, another one takes its place.

Perhaps the most important strategy for spouses is to not suffer alone. Friends and family members must be asked for all the help they can offer. It is embarrassing to have others know that your spouse is depressed. Embarrassment, however, is a much smaller price to pay than the agony of caregiver burnout.

The second strategy is to work with your spouse's mental health professional. Make sure that your voice is heard on a regular basis by the therapist. As you live with your spouse, you can supply information that the psychiatrist or psychotherapist needs to know. Your input will help accelerate the recovery process so that your spouse can get back to work and life.

The third strategy is to seek professional care for yourself. You may in fact be depressed as well and in need of your own treatment. A competent therapist will help you find ways to cope that may have eluded you so far.

No discussion of depression and marriage would be complete without mention of the negative impact of depression on marital intimacy. Depression always interferes in this area, and antidepressant medications may interfere as well. Speak with your therapist about concerns that you have. Shame or embarrassment will only get in the way of getting helpful guidance.

Depression is hard on any marriage. Tempers may run short as energy wanes. It is not uncommon for couples to feel as though their marriage is falling apart. Whether or not it actually is is beside the point. Until your spouse has resumed functioning as he or she once did, your marriage will be under stress. While one of you is depressed, discussion about the future of your life together should be "out of bounds."

The good news is that many marriages have weathered the depression of a spouse. Go easy on yourselves. Look for the good in each other. Use this trying time as an opportunity to strengthen the life-restoring skills of forgiveness, grace under fire, resilience, and humor. Ask Hashem for assistance and hope. You will not be disappointed.

Parenting While You Are Depressed

It is hardly a surprise that depression harshly interferes with your relationship with your children. The inner agony that you experience makes it difficult to attend to your children's multifaceted physical, emotional, educational, and spiritual needs. Regrettably, your failure to live up to the image of the kind of parent you wish to be feeds into your sense of failure.

This negative feedback is unwarranted. The fact is that you are clinically depressed. Part of the disease is the inability to put aside your pain. Part of the disease is to socially withdraw from others. Part of the disease is irritability and lowered frustration tolerance. These limitations are not you. Beating yourself up over letting your children down is not going to help you or your children.

What will help your children? How can children survive and thrive when a parent is clinically depressed? You'd be surprised to hear that children are much less harmed by parental depression than expected. Certainly it is a difficult passage for a child. But children have a remarkable resilience that buffers them. In the event that a child is having difficulty in school or with social skills, competent and compassionate psychotherapy can be of great help.

Nevertheless, it is vital that you do everything possible to accelerate your healing and recovery. While it is reasonable that you will be unable to parent your children like you did prior to your depression, this is not a license to lapse into a destructive state of self-pity and indulgence. Focus on practicing the recovery skills in this book. Keep your appointments. Take your medication. Nurture yourself and celebrate every single step of your recovery. Become a role model to your children by facing up to a problem that needs fixing. You will find unexpected *siyatta diShmaya* as you work on your program.

From the Author's Case Files

Miri contacted me following a lecture I had given in her shul. Over the phone she told me that her husband, Ari, had taken a leave of absence from his job because of his depression. Despite a whole cocktail of medications, he wasn't getting any better. She felt that there had to be a better way to get her husband up and moving again.

Miri and I scheduled a session together to figure out how we could help Ari. She gave me some background on his depression and his medications and told me that when the psychiatrist who had prescribed the medication recommended psychotherapy, Ari refused. She didn't know why he had refused, but she was pessimistic about changing his mind.

When I explained how Ari's ability to make any

decision, let alone a decision about medical treatment, was undermined by his depression, Miri immediately understood. I encouraged her to identify the reasons why she wanted Ari to come see me. She was then encouraged to write a letter to him. I suggested that she approach Ari with a choice: either she would read the letter to him or he would read it himself. I recommended that she choose a time of day when Ari's symptoms seemed to be their least intense.

I was quite straightforward with Miri: I told her that she had a right to demand that her husband seek treatment for his sake, for her sake, and for the sake of their five children. I also encouraged her to reassure Ari that she loved him and believed in his ability to make a decision that was right for the whole family.

Three days later I got a call from Ari. We set up an appointment. When we met, he told me that he had come to the realization that he needed some more help than his medications to get his life back. We examined his symptoms and how they were affecting his life and family. Ari had ongoing areas of dissatisfaction with his work and the death of his mother three years earlier. Nevertheless, it was apparent that his symptoms were less connected to any external events than they were to self-sabotaging mental habits.

We agreed to first focus on getting him moving again. In that first session we were able to begin setting up an activity schedule. Ari first wrote down those activities that he was already doing. I then asked him to think of one more activity that he could add to his repertoire. He told me that his son's school had started a new program of encouraging the seventh and eighth graders to go to maariv during the week. He wanted to go with his son to encourage him along. I thought that was an excellent idea. I pressed him to identify what obstacles he might encounter. He was able to name a few, such as shame, lethargy, and resistance to new undertakings. With further assistance he was able to think of some counters to those obstacles. I then sent him home after scheduling another appointment for four days later.

Ari came in the following week to report that he had indeed gone with his son to shul. He reported, however, that he still felt empty inside and could see little significance in this effort. I asked him what needed to change in order for him to be able to see the positive in himself. It was at that point that Ari began to open up about his self-loathing and his profound distrust of himself.

We both worked hard that session and the following session. Ari seemed to be catching on to the idea that his beliefs about himself were erroneous. He realized that he was in need of changing his mental habits. But how? Before introducing him to the strategies outlined in chapter 7, I suggested that his wife could be most helpful in this project. He agreed that the more people involved in his "mental remodeling" (his term), the faster it would go.

The next session, Ari, Miri, and I examined how Ari could effectively change the way he thought. We reviewed the strategies. I encouraged the two of them to figure out how Miri could help Ari without assuming the role of his therapist. They worked out an excellent plan between themselves. I continued to see Ari weekly *for another six sessions and then once a month for a year. Ari made a wonderful recovery. I think he has his wife to thank for that.*

Chapter 17

Special Concerns for Women

Women occupy a central role in the survival of the Jewish people. As mothers, prophets, teachers, and communal leaders, Jewish women are an unstoppable force. Unfortunately, however, in many ways women have special vulnerabilities to depression. Postpartum depression and perimenopausal depression are quite able to stop even the healthiest and strongest Jewish mothers. The good news is that treatment for these conditions really does help.

What Is Postpartum Depression?

The *Diagnostic and Statistical Manual* of the American Psychiatric Association states that postpartum depression (PPD) is a subtype of clinical depression that begins within one month of delivery. Some authorities believe that the window for developing PPD should be extended to a year after childbirth. PPD can occur whether the baby was born healthy and well or if, Heaven forbid, the baby did not survive. No matter what, the severity of

Special Concerns for Women

PPD far exceeds the minor mood disturbance known as the baby blues.

Scientists do not fully understand why some women get depressed after childbirth. Certainly the stress of being a new parent even if one has had children before can be a cause of PPD. There are so many dizzying and exhausting changes that must be taken into consideration. Yet the hormonal changes that occur in a woman after childbirth are so profound that scientists keep targeting those changes as being the central culprit in PPD.

The symptoms of PPD are much the same as those for clinical depression. In addition to those symptoms listed in chapter 1, many women with PPD report experiencing one or more of the following symptoms:

- Overconcern for the baby
- Uncontrollable crying
- Guilt, inadequacy, worthlessness
- Lack of interest in the baby
- Fear of harming the baby or oneself
- Fear of losing control or "going crazy"
- Exaggerated highs and lows
- Lack of interest in marital intimacy
- Intrusive or disturbing thoughts

How Often Does PPD Occur?

Scientists differ on the rate of occurrence. The most accepted estimate is ten percent of mothers. The greatest risk of developing PPD is among women who have had clinical depression in the past. Complicated family situations such as unemployment, poverty, illness, and absence of support increase the risk even more.

Treatment of PPD

This book emphasizes treatment of clinical depression that balances psychology and biology. Postpartum depression is an important exception to this approach. The first stop for curing PPD is most often your local druggist. Whereas other types of depression respond equally well to medication or cognitive psychotherapy, psychotherapy should not be relied upon to the exclusion of medication for PPD. Family members who suspect that a new mother is showing signs of PPD should encourage her to meet with a gynecologist or competent psychiatrist.

This scientifically based standard of care may have important ramifications for women who have decided to nurse their infants. Organizations such as La Leche League have made wonderful strides in encouraging women to nurse their children. Yet many women who are in desperate need of antidepressant medication refuse to take the medication because they are lactating.

The fact is that some antidepressants may be safely used while a woman is nursing without any harm to the infant or mother. However, in a misguided attempt to seek relief from their postpartum depression without medication, women will often enter psychotherapy or experiment with all sorts of untested homeopathic remedies. This allegiance to nursing is not only misguided but dangerous as well.

The centrality of medication should not, however, take away from the importance of psychotherapy when needed. Medication will not alleviate marital conflict, unemployment, grief from fetal death, or other stresses that exacerbate PPD. In such situations competent and compassionate psychotherapy can make all the difference in the world.

On the Topic of Postpartum

Postpartum depression is unfortunately not the only childbirth related psychiatric illness that affects women. Despite the joy and excitement of pregnancy, pregnant women may become even severely depressed and anxious. Following childbirth women can develop severe forms of anxiety disorders such as obsessive compulsive disorder, bipolar disorder, and postpartum psychosis. The latter can have extremely tragic consequences. For this reason family and friends are well advised to encourage new mothers who are exhibiting disturbing changes in behavior to see a psychiatrist. Once she is in treatment, continued support and encouragement are invaluable to successful cure.

What Is Perimenopausal Depression?

As a woman's childbearing years wind down there are dramatic changes occurring in her body. The most well-known changes involve hormonal regulation and menstruation. The trickle-down effect of these hormonal changes is vast. Skin, bones, heart, and all internal organs are affected by the ebb and flow of menopause.

Predictably, these changes affect mood regulation as

well. Women during and after menopause complain of mood swings, memory disturbances, loss of interest in marital relations, and sleep difficulties. For many years scientists and physicians attributed the depression of perimenopausal women to a psychological reaction to this physical change of life. Depressed perimenopausal women were once dismissed as hysteric, neurotic, psychotic, or all of the above.

The scientific community has now come to realize that psychology may play a much more limited role in this type of depression. Neuroscientists have increasingly focused on the depletion of essential hormones such as estrogen and testosterone as the force that drives these disturbing symptoms. In many cases antidepressants are relatively useless without the addition of some form of hormone replacement therapy. This speaks to the centrality of the changes in a woman's physiology in depression during menopause.

Little is known about the rate of occurrence of perimenopausal depression. It is quite accepted that women who have had an episode of clinical depression or postpartum depression are at increased risk. And, as with postpartum depression, the first stop for relief must be medication. Because of the well-known controversies surrounding hormone replacement, it is important to seek the assistance of a competent gynecologist along with a qualified psychiatrist.

Chapter 18

Special Concerns for Men

Men have occupied a central role throughout the glorious history of the Jewish people. As fathers, teachers, sages, philosophers, leaders, and warriors, Jewish men have excelled in the most important roles in *Yiddishkeit*. Unfortunately, men also have unique vulnerabilities to clinical depression. Conflicting cultural demands and excessive levels of stress in today's world conspire to undermine the joy in living for many male members of the Torah community.

There is good news, though. More and more Torah-observant men are seeking professional help for their depressions. Researchers have identified many of the unique social, psychological, and physiological factors that are to blame in male depression. This chapter will describe those vulnerabilities that are unique to men. Most importantly, it will confront the shame that prevents so many Torah-observant men from getting the help they need.

How Culture Makes Men Vulnerable to Depression

Despite our best efforts to keep it out, secular Western culture has made inroads into the lifestyle of many Torah Jews. One of the worst manifestations of the permeation of Western culture is materialism. Western culture views material possessions as a barometer of personal worth. The more you have, the more you are worth. Devotion to kindness and service of Hashem are of secondary value.

Regrettably many men, even fine *bnei Torah* and *baalei batim*, have been influenced by this destructive value system. Many of us judge others and ourselves by the ever-expanding measure of net-worth. Since the "acceptable" measure of net-worth continues to climb, men often feel as though they cannot keep up. Such a lifestyle is a recipe for demoralization. Chronic demoralization is the ideal environment for the development of depression.

Consider the words of Chaim, a forty-two-year-old pediatrician, husband, and father of six:

> *When I became frum after college one of the things that attracted me to Yiddishkeit was the rejection of the materialism that I had grown up with. So here I am twenty years later, living in a Torah community, and I see the same materialism that I wanted to get away from. And I am not innocent, either. Sometimes I catch myself feeling jealous of members of my community who have fancy cars and homes. When I feel that way I get angry at myself and everyone else. I have to work hard to be grateful to Hashem and focus on what I have and not*

Special Concerns for Men

on what I don't have and don't need.

Furthermore, from childhood, boys in Western culture are discouraged from the full range of emotional expression. While toughness is valued and the expression of anger is permitted in men, the free expression of sadness and emotional vulnerability are prohibited. Regardless of what feelings are permitted, boys and men experience all feelings, even those associated with femininity. Yet boys and men become ashamed of themselves when belittled by parents, teachers, and society for having "undesirable" feelings such as sadness and fear. Shame, like demoralization, is a potent breeding ground for male depression.

Consider the words of Yitzchak, a forty-eight-year-old shul rabbi, husband, and father of five:

> *The last few years of my rabbanus have been grueling. There was a major dispute within the shul that I think caused my depression. My internist encouraged me to find a therapist to talk things over with. Among the issues that came up was my difficulty with expressing feelings that I didn't like. My wife or parents would ask me how I was feeling and I would say, "Fine," even though I was dying inside. I was worried that I would be dismissed and that the fight would last forever. I knew that being honest with my feelings would help, but I was just too afraid of looking weak. The therapist helped me feel more comfortable with my feelings when he pointed out that David HaMelech was very open with his feelings.*

Finally, there is no avoiding the fact that men in the Torah community are under tremendous stress. Skyrocketing costs of raising a Torah family have put great pressure on men who bear most of the responsibility for generating their families' income. Jam-packed schedules make it almost impossible for men to find time to relax, maintain a nutritious diet, and exercise. This lifestyle makes many men vulnerable to clinical depression.

How Physiology Makes Men Vulnerable to Depression

In recent years evidence has emerged that men's unique physiology may add a unique vulnerability. Testosterone has been often found to be significantly lower in men suffering from depression. A major depression researcher, Harrison Pope, urges men who have not responded to antidepressant medication to get their testosterone level checked.

The jury is still out regarding the relationship between testosterone and depression. Yet the fact that the introduction of synthetic testosterone has helped boost the moods of depressed men indicates that male hormones are involved in depression. With more research a definitive relationship will come into sharper focus.

The Differences between Male Depression and Female Depression

The symptoms of depression listed in the *Diagnostic and Statistical Manual* of the American Psychiatric Association apply to both men and women. Nevertheless, men tend to experience depression differently than many woman do. Men tend to complain about sleep difficulties and physical aches and pains more than women do. Men also mask their depression with uncharacteristic irritability, loss of interest in activities that they previously enjoyed, and social withdrawal. In severe states of depression, men are much more likely to successfully commit suicide than women.

Consider the words of Moshe, a fifty-three-year-old lawyer, husband, and father of five children.

> *During a lengthy trial I kept feeling sick. It seemed as though I was running off to my internist for one problem or another. One time I was in such a rush to get in to see him and then get back to my office that I lost my temper with his receptionist. My doctor, who had known me since we were in college together, told me he was worried about me. He said that all of the uncharacteristic illnesses and my tirade turned on a lightbulb in his head. He suggested that I see a psychiatrist whose office was next door. At first I told him that he was crazy, but then we talked for a bit. He pointed out some things that I had overlooked.*
>
> *I made an appointment with the psychiatrist. He recommended some medication and a few sessions of therapy. I am feeling much better now, baruch Hashem.*

Getting Your Life Back

It is not easy being a depressed male. All sorts of forces conspire to make it difficult to get the help that men need and deserve. Nevertheless, halachah and common sense demand an honest acceptance of depression and the need for treatment. The consistent use of the strategies in *Returning to Joy* will help you enjoy your life once again.

Untreated depression destroys lives and families. The shame and embarrassment that prevents you from seeking help reflects a distortion of Torah priorities. In recent years many famous men in secular society have publicly come forward with their stories of recovery from crippling depression. The journalist Mike Wallace, the writer William Styron, the football hero Terry Bradshaw are a few examples of such celebrities who have shared their struggles with the public. *B'nei Torah* too can learn to disregard public judgment and get the help that they need.

Chapter 19

Depression and the Torah-Observant Single

Singles are not immune to depression and its devastating symptoms. Because of the unique pressures a single Torah-observant Jew encounters, he or she has unique vulnerabilities to depression. One such pressure is in the nature of *shidduchim*.

When one goes on a job interview, all that is judged is his ability to perform the expected tasks. When you go on a *shidduch* date you are judged in many different and intimate areas. This includes your appearance, spirituality, and social graces, as well as the pedigree of your family. While this system has many advantages, the pressurized nature makes it very hard on some young adults. This is particularly the case when one is depressed, anxious, ashamed, or having difficulties with self-esteem. Rejection can send a vulnerable person into a nosedive.

In order to escape this pressure, singles may feel

compelled to make choices that have lifelong impact. And because depression distorts self-esteem, depressed singles may be very prone to making disastrous marital choices.

Because of this vulnerability, it may be recommended that the single take a brief hiatus from dating. This break gives the individual time to focus on recovering his or her emotional health. Before taking this break, it is wise to ask the advice of a knowledgeable rabbi. No matter what, the fear of missing your *bashert* must not intrude on one's recovery from depression. Having treated many single Torah-observant Jews for depression, I know that they can get married. I even have the wedding invitations to prove it!

Disclosing depression is a sensitive matter. Such an important issue should be discussed with a trusted rabbi. Suffice it to say that a healthy relationship is founded on honesty. Failing to disclose any health problem such as depression or diabetes is an unforgivable deception. Nevertheless, because of the stigma associated depression, disclosure is not a simple matter. Discuss it with your rabbi and therapist.

From the Author's Case Files

Esti was twenty-three years old when I first met her. She was suffering from depression and had been referred to me by a psychiatrist who knew of my work with depressed young adults. Realizing that she was also extremely troubled by the looming issue of marriage, he encouraged her to get some psychotherapy in addition to taking medication.

Indeed, the issues of marriage and dating figured

Depression and the Torah-Observant Single

significantly in Esti's depression. Her family and seminary teachers had been badgering her to get married for the last year, and she also wanted to be married already. However, all of this external and internal pressure was leading to a demoralized young woman. In her current state, she was opposed to going on shidduchim but didn't have the psychological energy to tell her well-meaning shadchanim that she needed a breather. Her worry that she would miss her bashert made it even more difficult for her to think of taking a break.

Esti agreed with me that her depressed mood and ways of thinking were interfering with her life. She knew that she had difficulty thinking clearly. She agreed that a businessperson in such a state would probably be unable to do his or her job. And while she was somewhat hesitant to make the same connection to dating, she did agree to meet with a rabbi who we both agreed could give helpful advice.

At the session following the meeting with the rabbi, Esti told me that he thought that a three-month break from shidduchim was in order. He urged Esti to use this hiatus to strengthen her self-confidence. He also reassured her that Hashem would help her meet her zivug once she was ready.

Esti told me that she was somewhat surprised by his recommendation. She had assumed that he would dismiss any mental health concerns that we had discussed. This "surprise" initiated an important exploration of the toxic cognitive spices of depression.

Esti learned to become more vigilant of her habit of jumping to conclusions that robbed her of hope. She kept a journal of her feelings and learned to celebrate herself.

She made excellent use of her therapy and the breather recommended by her rabbi. When she resumed dating she was confident in herself and in her future. It didn't take long for her to meet a young man who appreciated her for who she was. That was a wedding I was thrilled to attend.

Chapter 20
The Older Adult and Depression

We are told in *Pirkei Avos* (5:21) that the ages of seventy and eighty are periods of great wisdom and strength. In the Torah view, the older years are to be filled with a level of vigor not available to the younger person. In authentic Jewish culture older people occupy central places in the community. They live out the remainder of their lives surrounded by family and loved ones, reaping the earthly rewards of lives well lived.

Unfortunately, this ideal is more often the exception than the rule. Older adults have been pushed aside. Western culture's obsession with youth has resulted in shunning the older members of society. Retirement often severs the individual from the profession that has given him or her status and meaning over the years.

Because of these and other factors, depression in older adults is rampant. The *Diagnostic and Statistical Manual* of the American Psychiatric Association reports that between 25 and 50 percent of older adults are clinically depressed.

The consequences of older adult depression are devastating. Physical health declines much more rapidly. Mental awareness fades as the older adult recedes from life into his own inner misery. Years that could be spent enjoying time with family and spiritual fulfillment become filled with misery.

The Unique Signs of Depression in the Older Adult

Depression in the older adult can manifest itself differently than it would in younger people. While some older adults may openly complain of sadness, many simply deny feeling depressed. Instead, they will become uncharacteristically withdrawn or irritable. The depressed older adult may stop eating and report that he or she is not sleeping well. Preoccupation with vague complaints of pain that are not relieved by regular medical intervention can be signs of depression.

How Family and Friends Can Help

Family members and friends are usually the ones who first detect depression in the older adult. The proper response to it can sometimes be somewhat thorny. Obviously, the best way is to gently raise your concerns with your loved one. Just as often as people responded with denial or minimization, they respond with gratitude for having the issue brought up. When a depressed older adult responds with openness, you can further help him by helping him find a competent and compassionate professional who can effectively work with him to relieve this depression.

When, however, your concerns are met with anger

or disregard, a straightforward approach will most often fail. Instead, consider sharing concerns with an individual who is respected by the older adult. A rabbi or physician can often intervene much more easily without arousing all sorts of resistance.

When helping the older adult find a mental health professional, it is vital to select candidates who have training and experience in the treatment of depression in older adults. While all psychiatrists can legally prescribe medications for any patient, geriatric psychiatrists are specially trained for this population.

Older adults often have medical conditions that negatively effect their mood. They may be taking many different types of medications which alone or in combination may undermine their mental health. Because depression can interfere with memory and concentration, many depressed older adults are often misdiagnosed as having some form of dementia. For this reason it is vital to help the older adult work with a professional who is sensitive to the special needs and assets of the patient.

From the Author's Case Files

During the lunch break in a workshop on mental health several years ago, I was approached by a woman who asked if I could find a few minutes to speak with her. I finished my lunch and went over to the woman's table.

The woman, Carol, quickly got down to business. Her mother, Sylvia, then seventy-nine years old, had just started attending an intense outpatient psychiatric program at a hospital near where I used to live. Carol asked me about the program and whether I thought it could meet her mother's needs. Wanting to address the issue in the most accurate manner, I asked Carol some questions about her mother.

Carol told me that two weeks before she had come to her mother's apartment and found her gasping for breath, confused, and almost incoherent. Carol immediately called her mother's doctor, who directed her to take Sylvia to the local emergency room. Sylvia was seen immediately by a doctor, who ran a battery of tests and stated that there was no medical cause for these symptoms. Deciding that she was having a panic attack, he prescribed a common tranquilizer. There appeared to be some improvement, but the doctor felt that an overnight hospitalization was in order. Just to make sure that everything was okay, he said.

Unfortunately, the following morning Sylvia was still significantly confused. The attending doctor believed that a psychiatric consultation was in order. A psychiatrist was summoned and after a brief interview decided that Sylvia was probably depressed. He wrote out a prescription for a well-known antidepressant and recommended that Sylvia set up an appointment with his office for the following week. Sylvia was then discharged from the hospital.

Despite a definite feeling that there was something missing in all that had transpired, Carol took her mother to the doctor's appointment. Again the doctor spent very little time speaking with Sylvia. He decided to double the dose of medication and he insisted that Sylvia return for another appointment the next week. By the time Sylvia's second appointment came around, she was agitated and miserable. She had insomnia and her appetite was terrible. This usually serene and pa-

The Older Adult and Depression

tient woman was irritable. The psychiatrist decided that Sylvia needed to attend a daily outpatient psychiatric program, the one that Carol was now asking me about.

"Whoa," I exclaimed, my eyes wide with incredulity. "Did your mother ever have depression?"

"No," answered Carol.

"Did you notice your mother's mood deteriorate over the week or two prior to that trip to the emergency room?"

"Well, she had been somewhat edgy and less patient than normal. My son told me that she had yelled at him when he visited her."

"Was there any external factor that may have disturbed your mother? The death of a friend? Financial problems?"

"No, except she was complaining about the fact that she had not regained her strength from a respiratory infection."

"Oh, she had a respiratory infection. Was she given any medication for it?"

"Of course! Her internist gave her some antibiotics and some medication to help her breathing."

As soon as Carol said that, the hair on the back of my head stood on end. I knew the medication even before she told me which it was. I told Carol that she must get her mother back to her internist immediately because the medication that he was prescribing was well known for causing mood instability and anxiety.

A week later I received a phone call from a very grateful Carol. She told me that she brought Sylvia to the doctor that afternoon and he could not believe what *she had gone through. He stopped her respiratory medications and lowered the dose of the antidepressant medication. The three of them agreed that if Sylvia remained depressed and anxiety ridden then she would consult with a geriatric psychiatrist who was well regarded in the community. But, Carol told me, that was unnecessary, as within a day of stopping the medication her mother was back to her patient and serene self.*

Conclusion

The Gift of Clinical Depression

Why did Hashem make it appear to the Jewish people that Pharaoh was gaining on them as they approached the Sea of Reeds?

Rabbi Yehoshua ben Levi said: The matter is similar to the following parable. A king was traveling on a highway when he encountered a princess crying out, "I beg of you, save me from these robbers." The king saved her and brought her to his palace. After a few days he wished to marry her. He wished that she would speak with him, but she refused. What did the king do? He instigated the robbers to attack her in order that she would call out for help. As soon as she saw the robbers, she began to plead for assistance. The king then said to her, "All I wanted was to hear your voice." So too, Hashem wanted only to hear the prayers of the Jewish people. He therefore showed them Pharaoh.

(*Midrash Rabbah, Beshalach* 21)

Returning to Joy has focused on the destructive aspects of depression. Depression distorts how we see reality, how we feel, how we think, and how we act. Depression is responsible for broken marriages and families. Indeed, the damage caused by depression is incalculable.

Nevertheless, our awareness of God's role as Creator and Sustainer of the Universe includes the willingness to understand that there is another side to depression. Everything that God has created and will create is good. That includes clinical depression. While I cannot speak for others, here are two ways that I view clinical depression as a gift without which humanity would be much worse off.

Depression is a reminder that we all need each other. It is the ultimate equalizer. No one is immune to depression. Rich people get depressed. Strong people get depressed. Attractive people get depressed. No matter how independent a person may believe him or herself, he or she is still vulnerable. And because we are vulnerable, we need others to help lead us out of the darkness of depression.

Depression keeps us on track about what is truly important in life. Most people in treatment for depression begin to feel better when they start making positive changes in their life. Perhaps they have begun reaching out to people. Perhaps they have begun to debate their dark, pessimistic beliefs. Perhaps they have made some improvements in their health habits. Without depression, however, they would have not made those changes.

Whether you have found the gift in depression or not, these gifts are there. As you use the strategies contained in *Returning to Joy*, these blessings will become manifest. You will appreciate fully the conclusion of the verse discussed in the beginning of this book, "Release my soul from the trap...in order that the righteous shall use me as a crown to adorn themselves."

Appendix A

List of Feelings

Abandoned	Blah	Deprived
Accepted	Boastful	Despairing
Accepting	Boisterous	Despised
Accomplished	Bored	Despising
Achy	Bossy	Detached
Afraid	Burned out	Different
Aggravated	Calm	Diffident
Agitated	Capable	Dirty
Amazed	Charitable	Disabled
Ambitious	Comfortable	Disappointed
Ambivalent	Competent	Disbelieving
Amused	Confident	Disconnected
Angry	Conflicted	Disgusted
Annoyed	Confused	Disheveled
Antisocial	Courageous	Displeased
Anxious	Cowardly	Disregarded
Apprehensive	Crabby	Disrespected
Aroused	Cranky	Disrespectful
Asinine	Criticized	Disturbed
Bashful	Cunning	Doubting
Beautiful	Curious	Educated
Betrayed	Defeated	Embarrassed

RETURNING TO JOY

Empty	Hopeful	Naïve
Energetic	Hopeless	Odd
Energized	Humiliated	Oppressed
Enraged	Hungry	Optimistic
Enthusiastic	Ignored	Overjoyed
Envious	Ignoring	Overprotected
Euphoric	Impatient	Overwhelmed
Excited	Inadequate	Paranoid
Exhausted	Indifferent	Pathetic
Exploited	Indignant	Peaceful
Explosive	Inept	Pessimistic
Faithful	Inferior	Plain
Fat	Infuriated	Pleased
Fatigued	Interested	Poor
Fearful	Invisible	Powerful
Fed up	Irritable	Powerless
Flamboyant	Irritated	Quiet
Flat	Jealous	Ravenous
Frustrated	Joyous	Receptive
Furious	Left out	Rejected
Generous	Listless	Rejuvenated
Giddy	Lonely	Relaxed
Gracious	Loved	Reluctant
Grateful	Loyal	Resentful
Grumpy	Lucky	Reserved
Guilty	Lustful	Respected
Gutsy	Mean	Respectful
Happy	Mischievous	Restless
Hated	Misunderstood	Righteous
Hateful	Modest	Sad
Helpful	Mortified	Sarcastic
Helpless	Murderous	Satisfied

List of Feelings

Scared	Superior	Unassuming
Secure	Surprised	Uncomfortable
Serene	Suspicious	Understood
Sheepish	Swindled	Undeserving
Shocked	Taken	Uneasy
Shy	Tense	Unheard
Silly	Terrified	Unimportant
Sleepy	Ticked off	Unloved
Slow	Timid	Unsatisfied
Smart	Tired	Untrusting
Social	Tormented	Unworthy
Spooked	Torn	Validated
Stifled	Touchy	Valued
Stimulated	Treated unfairly	Violated
Stressed	Tricked	Vulnerable
Strong	Trusting	Wary
Stubborn	Trustworthy	Weak
Stunned	Turned on	Weepy
Stupid	Unaccomplished	Welcomed
Successful	Unappreciated	

Appendix B

Antidepressant Medications

The following is a list of antidepressant medications that are prescribed by physicians for the treatment of depression. These medications have been primarily used for the treatment of clinical depression. In the United States they have received the approval of the Federal Drug Administration (FDA) for the treatment of depression. Many of them have been rigorously studied and used for the treatment of other disorders as well. Some of these uses have been approved by the FDA; some have not.

The list is not complete for two reasons. First, new medications are entering the marketplace constantly. Second, old medications are often being reformulated so that they may have new names. Any list of medications is therefore going to be outdated quickly.

Medications are also called by different names in different places. The brand names commonly used in the United States are often not the same as brand names in Israel or Europe. While the chemical name, commonly referred to as the generic name, is usually the same regardless of location, this is not always the case.

Antidepressant Medications

For this reason this list is not fully comprehensive.

This list uses the most common classification system to organize these medications. These classes are selective serotonin reuptake inhibitors, selective noradrenaline reuptake inhibitor, tricylclic antidepressants, and bupropion. Scientists have not been able to unequivocally explain how these medications relieve the symptoms of depression. Hypotheses have been offered. Only time and continued research will tell. Nevertheless, a concise summary of the dominant theory accompanies each class of antidepressant medication.

Selective Serotonin Reuptake Inhibitors (SSRI'S)

Serotonin is a neurotransmitter made by the cells in the brain. SSRI antidepressants slow the rate that the brain breaks down serotonin. This in turn causes an increase in serotonin activity in the parts of the brain involved in mood regulation and decision making. This has been shown to improve symptoms of depression.

COMMON BRAND NAME	GENERIC NAME
Prozac; Lovan	Fluoxetine
Zoloft	Sertraline
Aropax, Paxil	Paroxetine
Cipramil; Celexa; Recital	Citalopram
Luvox	Fluvoxamine

Selective Noradrenaline Reuptake Inhibitors (SNRI's)

Noradrenaline is another brain neurotransmitter. It is believed to be responsible for the regulation of mood and physical energy levels. SNRI antidepressants slow the rate that the brain breaks down serotonin and noradrenaline. This leads to an increase in serotonin and noradrenaline activity in the regions of the brain that are believed to be responsible for mood regulation.

COMMON BRAND NAME	GENERIC NAME
Effexor	Venlafaxine
Serzone	Nefazadone
Remeron	Mirtazapine (closely related but not identical to SNRI)

Tricyclic Antidepressants

Tricyclic antidepressants have been used for more than 40 years. The tricyclic antidepressants increase the amount of noradrenaline and serotonin in the brain. This, in turn, enhances the mood regulation system of the parts of the brain affected by depression. (See chart on the facing page.)

Bupropion

There are two brand names associated with the bupropion class of antidepressants. They are Wellbutrin and Zyban. It is believed that bupropion works by preventing the reuptake and breaking down of dopamine, a neurotransmitter often associated with feelings of pleasure.

Antidepressant Medications

COMMON BRAND NAME	CHEMICAL NAME
Tryptanol; Endep	Amitriptyline
Tofranil; Melipramine	Imipramine
Prothiaden; Dothep	Dothiepin
Allegron	Nortriptyline
Surmontil	Trimipramine
Anafranil; Placil; Clopram	Clomipramine
Sinequan; Deptran	Doxepin

Appendix C
Electroconvulsive Therapy

One of the most controversial aspects of clinical depression is the use of electroconvulsive therapy (ECT). ECT evokes strong reactions among patients, laypeople, and professionals alike. In the minds of many people, ECT is a barbaric pseudotreatment that has no place in a modern discussion of clinical depression.

The facts, however, do not support this stereotype. Many patients who have not benefited from medication therapy or psychotherapy have benefited immensely from ECT. Scientists have found a 90-percent cure rate with ECT. Aside from a brief period of amnesia before and after the procedure, there are no side effects to ECT. It is a particularly safe procedure for older patients. Since the popular antidepressant medications can have a variety of side effects, ECT is certainly the safer bet.

Contrary to the popular misconception, the ECT procedure does not involve a Dr. Frankenstein–like blasting of electric sparks. The whole procedure is con-

Electroconvulsive Therapy

ducted in a relaxed and quiet atmosphere. An anesthesiologist sedates the patient. Eighty volts of current are then applied to the patient's head. This causes a mild seizure. In this seizure state, the brain is flooded with neurotransmitters, which induce a chemical "reset." When the patient emerges from the seizure, he or she often feels better. The whole procedure is over in a matter of minutes. Most patients need only one procedure. Some may require more. The procedure is always conducted in a hospital.

Unfortunately, because of the stigma associated with ECT it is not as available as it should be. Few hospitals offer ECT. Most psychiatrists are not trained in the administration of ECT. If you believe that ECT may be for you, ask your mental health professional for assistance in locating a hospital and psychiatrist who can help you.

Appendix D
Psychosis and Depression

All depression involves some loss of touch with reality. Even a mildly depressed person dismisses clear-cut evidence that he or she is not as much a failure as he or she may believe. Yet scientists would never consider such faulty reasoning as psychotic.

There are situations, however, when severe depression is accompanied by profound loss of touch with reality or psychosis. Severely depressed patients may falsely report that they have committed some unspeakable crime. They may report hearing voices that tell them over and over how evil they are. They may wander about or sit unresponsively for hours in a corner. Attempts to reason with a psychotically depressed patient or change his behavior almost always fails.

Depression with psychosis is one of the most dangerous forms of the disease. With good reason, mental health professionals are trained to respond forcefully when a patient becomes psychotic. Antipsychotic medication may be recommended to help relieve the psycho-

Psychosis and Depression

sis. If the patient is at risk of suicide or unable to care for himself or herself, hospitalization is needed. The good news is that with the proper care psychotic depressions appear to clear rapidly.

For Further Reading

Here is a list of excellent books on overcoming depression.

- *Learned Optimism: How to Change Your Mind and Your Life.* Martin Seligman, New York: Simon & Schuster, 1998.

This book is a modern-day classic of common sense and scientific research. Martin Seligman and his associates have invested decades of research in developing the most effective ways to help people think clearly.

- *Depression Workbook: A Guide for Living with Depression and Manic Depression.* Mary Ellen Copeland. Oakland, CA: New Harbinger Publications, 2001.

This is an excellent source of guidance for living with chronic depression. Mary Ellen Copeland candidly describes her own story of coping with decades of crippling depression. Even better, she shared tips that have worked for her and for thousands of others in finding life in the midst of depression.

- *Breaking the Patterns of Depression.* Michael Yapko. New York: Broadway Books, 1998.

For Further Reading

This book examines clinical depression as a combination of psychology, physiology, and social skills. It has some excellent chapters on changing self-sabotaging social habits.

- *Women's Moods, Women's Minds: What Every Woman Must Know about Hormones, the Brain, and Emotional Health.* Deborah Sichel and Jeanne Watson Driscoll. New York: Morrow, William, and Co., 2000. A must read for women of every age. It is well written and loaded with up-to-date research on women's mental health.

- *Mind Over Mood.* Dennis Greenberger and Christine A. Padesky. New York: Guilford Publications, 1995.

A classic. This book is based on the cognitive psychotherapy of depression of Dr. Aaron Beck. It focuses on changing the depressive patterns of thinking.

- *Emotional Maturity Established through Torah.* Miriam Adahan. Jerusalem: Feldheim Publishers, 1987.

A wonderful resource that is brimming with excellent techniques for managing destructive thoughts and feelings. *EMMET* has many sources that Torah-observant Jews will identify with.

- *Tehillim*

Whatever version you use or schedule you follow, *Tehillim* will always help you reconnect to hope. Keep it close by at all times.

About the Author

Rabbi Dr. Joshua Mark, Ph.D., has worked as a psychotherapist and clinical researcher for the last fifteen years. He has helped thousands of individuals find joy and fulfillment in their lives. Because of his warmth and straightforward approach to the concerns of the Torah community, he is a much sought-after speaker. Rabbi Dr. Mark practices psychotherapy in Raanana, Israel, where he lives with his family. You can learn more about Dr. Mark at his website, www.counselingexcellence.com.